THE ANNOTATED LUTHER STUDY EDITION

Treatise on Good Works

1520

THE ANNOTATED LUTHER STUDY EDITION

Treatise on Good Works

1520

TIMOTHY J. WENGERT

Fortress Press
Minneapolis

Treatise on Good Works, 1520
THE ANNOTATED LUTHER STUDY EDITION

Copyright © 2016 Fortress Press. All rights reserved. Except for brief quotations in critical articles
and reviews, no part of this book may be reproduced in any manner without prior written permission
from the publisher. Visit http://www.augsburgfortress.org/copyrights/contact.asp or write to
Permissions, Augsburg Fortress, Box 1209, Minneapolis, MN 55440.

Unless otherwise noted, Scripture quotations are from New Revised Standard Version Bible,
copyright © 1989 by the Division of Education of the National Council of Churches of Christ
in the United States of America.

Excerpted from The Annotated Luther, Volume 1, *The Roots of Reform*
(Minneapolis: Fortress Press, 2015), Timothy J. Wengert, volume editor.

Fortress Press Publication Staff:
Scott Tunseth, Project Editor
Marissa Wold Uhrina, Production Manager
Laurie Ingram, Cover Design
Esther Diley, Permissions

Copyeditor: David Lott
Series design and typesetting: Ann Delgehausen, Trio Bookworks
Proofreader: Laura Weller

Library of Congress Cataloging-in-Publication Data is available

Print ISBN: 978-1-5064-1353-2
eISBN: 978-1-5064-1354-9

The paper used in this publication meets the minimum requirements of American National Standard
for Information Sciences—Permanence of Paper for Printed Library Materials, ANSI Z329, 48-1984.

Manufactured in the U.S.A.

Contents

Publisher's Note

About the Annotated Luther Study Edition

The volumes in the Annotated Luther Study Edition series have first been published in one of the comprehensive volumes of The Annotated Luther series. A description of that series and the volumes can be found in the Series Introduction (p. vii). While each comprehensive Annotated Luther volume can easily be used in classroom settings, we also recognize that treatises are often assigned individually for reading and study. To facilitate classroom and group use, we have pulled key treatises along with their introductions, annotations, and images directly from the Annotated Luther Series volumes.

Please note that the study edition page numbers match the page numbers of the larger Annotated Luther volume in which it first appeared. We have intentionally retained the same page numbering to facilitate use of the study editions and larger volumes side by side.

Treatise on Good Works, 1520,
was first published in The Annotated Luther series,
Volume 1, *The Roots of Reform* (2015).

Series Introduction

Engaging the Essential Luther

Even after five hundred years Martin Luther continues to engage and challenge each new generation of scholars and believers alike. With 2017 marking the five-hundredth anniversary of Luther's *95 Theses*, Luther's theology and legacy are being explored around the world with new questions and methods and by diverse voices. His thought invites ongoing examination, his writings are a staple in classrooms and pulpits, and he speaks to an expanding assortment of conversation partners who use different languages and hale from different geographical and social contexts.

The six volumes of The Annotated Luther edition offer a flexible tool for the global reader of Luther, making many of his most important writings available in the *lingua franca* of our times as one way of facilitating interest in the Wittenberg reformer. They feature new introductions, annotations, revised translations, and textual notes, as well as visual enhancements (illustrations, art, photos, maps, and timelines). The Annotated Luther edition embodies Luther's own cherished principles of communication. Theological writing, like preaching, needs to reflect human beings' lived experience, benefits from up-to-date scholarship, and should be easily accessible to all. These volumes are designed to help teachers and students, pastors and laypersons, and other professionals in ministry understand the context in which the documents were written, recognize how the documents have shaped Protestant and Lutheran thinking, and interpret the meaning of these documents for faith and life today.

The Rationale for This Edition

For any reader of Luther, the sheer number of his works presents a challenge. Well over one hundred volumes comprise the scholarly edition of Luther's works, the so-called Weimar Ausgabe (WA), a publishing enterprise begun in 1883 and only completed in the twenty-first century. From 1955 to 1986, fifty-five volumes came to make up *Luther's Works* (American Edition) (LW), to which Concordia Publishing House, St. Louis, is adding still more. This English-language contribution to Luther studies, matched by similar translation projects for Erasmus of Rotterdam and John Calvin, provides a theological and historical gold mine for those interested in studying Luther's thought. But even these volumes are not always easy to use and are hardly portable. Electronic forms have increased availability, but preserving Luther in book form and providing readers with manageable selections are also important goals.

Moreover, since the publication of the WA and the first fifty-five volumes of the LW, research on the Reformation in general and on Martin Luther in particular has broken new ground and evolved, as has knowledge regarding the languages in which Luther wrote. Up-to-date information from a variety of sources is brought together in The Annotated Luther, building on the work done by previous generations of scholars. The language and phrasing of the translations have also been updated to reflect modern English usage. While the WA and, in a derivative way, LW remain the central source for Luther scholarship, the present critical and annotated English translation facilitates research internationally and invites a new generation of readers for whom Latin and German might prove an unsurpassable obstacle to accessing Luther. The WA provides the basic Luther texts (with some exceptions); the LW provides the basis for almost all translations.

Defining the "Essential Luther"

Deciding which works to include in this collection was not easy. Criteria included giving attention to Luther's initial key works; considering which publications had the most impact in his day and later; and taking account of Luther's own favorites, texts addressing specific issues of continued importance for today, and Luther's exegetical works. Taken as a whole, these works present the many sides of Luther, as reformer, pastor, biblical interpreter, and theologian. To serve today's readers and by using categories similar to those found in volumes 31–47 of Luther's works (published by Fortress Press), the volumes offer in the main a thematic rather than strictly chronological approach to Luther's writings. The volumes in the series include:

> Volume 1: *The Roots of Reform* (Timothy J. Wengert, editor)
> Volume 2: *Word and Faith* (Kirsi I. Stjerna, editor)
> Volume 3: *Church and Sacraments* (Paul W. Robinson, editor)
> Volume 4: *Pastoral Writings* (Mary Jane Haemig, editor)
> Volume 5: *Christian Life in the World* (Hans J. Hillerbrand, editor)
> Volume 6: *The Interpretation of Scripture* (Euan K. Cameron, editor)

The History of the Project

In 2011 Fortress Press convened an advisory board to explore the promise and parameters of a new English edition of Luther's essential works. Board members Denis Janz, Robert Kolb, Peter Matheson, Christine Helmer, and Kirsi Stjerna deliberated with

Fortress Press publisher Will Bergkamp to develop a concept and identify contributors. After a review with scholars in the field, college and seminary professors, and pastors, it was concluded that a single-language edition was more desirable than dual-language volumes.

In August 2012, Hans Hillerbrand, Kirsi Stjerna, and Timothy Wengert were appointed as general editors of the series with Scott Tunseth from Fortress Press as the project editor. The general editors were tasked with determining the contents of the volumes and developing the working principles of the series. They also helped with the identification and recruitment of additional volume editors, who in turn worked with the general editors to identify volume contributors. Mastery of the languages and unique knowledge of the subject matter were key factors in identifying contributors. Most contributors are North American scholars and native English speakers, but The Annotated Luther includes among its contributors a circle of international scholars. Likewise, the series is offered for a global network of teachers and students in seminary, university, and college classes, as well as pastors, lay teachers, and adult students in congregations seeking background and depth in Lutheran theology, biblical interpretation, and Reformation history.

Editorial Principles

The volume editors and contributors have, with few exceptions, used the translations of LW as the basis of their work, retranslating from the WA for the sake of clarity and contemporary usage. Where the LW translations have been substantively altered, explanatory notes have often been provided. More importantly, contributors have provided marginal notes to help readers understand theological and historical references. Introductions have been expanded and sharpened to reflect the very latest historical and theological research. In citing the Bible, care has been taken to reflect the German and Latin texts commonly used in the sixteenth century rather than modern editions, which often employ textual sources that were unavailable to Luther and his contemporaries.

Finally, all pieces in The Annotated Luther have been revised in the light of modern principles of inclusive language. This is not always an easy task with a historical author, but an intentional effort has been made to revise language throughout, with creativity and editorial liberties, to allow Luther's theology to speak free from unnecessary and unintended gender-exclusive language. This important principle provides an opportunity to translate accurately certain gender-neutral German and Latin expressions that Luther employed—for example, the Latin word *homo* and the German *Mensch* mean "human being," not simply "males." Using the words *man* and *men* to translate such terms would create an ambiguity not present in the original texts. The focus is on linguistic accuracy and Luther's intent. Regarding creedal formulations and trinitarian language, Luther's own expressions have been preserved, without entering the complex and important contemporary debates over language for God and the Trinity.

The 2017 anniversary of the publication of the *95 Theses* is providing an opportunity to assess the substance of Luther's role and influence in the Protestant Reformation. Revisiting Luther's essential writings not only allows reassessment of Luther's rationale and goals but also provides a new look at what Martin Luther was about and why new generations would still wish to engage him. We hope these six volumes offer a compelling invitation.

Hans J. Hillerbrand
Kirsi I. Stjerna
Timothy J. Wengert
General Editors

Abbreviations

ANF	*The Ante-Nicene Fathers: Translations of the Fathers down to A.D. 325.* 10 vols. Reprint, Grand Rapids: Eerdmans, 1978
Ap	*Apology of the Augsburg Confession*
BC	*The Book of Concord*, ed. Robert Kolb and Timothy J. Wengert (Minneapolis: Fortress Press, 2000).
BSLK	*Die Bekenntnichriften der evngelich-lutherichen Kirche.* 11th ed. (Gottingen: Vandenhoeck & Ruprecht, 1992).
CA	*Augsburg Confession (Confessio Augustana)*
CR	*Corpus Reformatorum: Philippi Melanthonis opera quae supersunt omnia*, ed. Karl Brettschneider and Heinrich Bindseil, 28 vols. (Braunschweig: Schwetchke, 1834-1860).
CSEL	*Corpus Scriptorum Ecclesiasticorum Latinorum (CSEL)*, 99 vols. 1866-2011.
CWE	*Spirituality: Enchiridon/De contemptu mundi/Devidua christiana*, vol. 66 (University of Toronto Press, 1988), 39.
Ep	*Epitome of the Formula of Concord*
FC	*Formula of Concord*
LC	*Large Catechism*
LW	*Luther's Works* [American edition], ed. Helmut Lehmann and Jaroslav Pelikan, 55 vols. (Philadelphia: Fortress Press/St. Louis: Concordia Publishing House, 1955-1986).
MLStA	*Martin Luther: Studienausgabe*, ed. Hans-Ulrich Delius, 6 vols. (Berlin/Leipzig: Evangelische Verlagsanstalt, 1979-1999).
MPG	*Patrologiae Cursus Completus, Series Graeca*, ed. J. P. Migne, 61 vols., (Paris, 1857-1912).
MPL	*Patrologiae cursus completus, series Latina*, ed. Jacques-Paul Migne, 217 vols. (Paris, 1815-1875).
NPNF	*Nicene and Post-Nicene Fathers*, ed. Philip Schaaf and Henry Wace, series 1, 14 vols.; and series 2, 14 vols. (London/New York: T&T Clark, 1886-1900).
OHMLT	*The Oxford Handbook of Martin Luther's Theology*, eds. Robert Kolb, Irene Dingel, and L'ubomír Batka (New York: Oxford University Press, 2015)
SA	*Smalcald Articles*
SBOp	Sancti Bernardi Opera 3 (Rome: Editiones Cistercienses, 1963).
SD	*Solid Declaration of the Formula of Concord*
STh	*Summa Theologica*
TAL	*The Annotated Luther*, vols. 1-6 (Minneapolis: Fortress Press, 2015-2017).
Tr	*Treatise on the Power and Primacy of the Pope*

WA   Luther, Martin. *Luthers Werke: Kritische Gesamtausgabe [Schriften]*,
            73 vols. (Weimar: H. Böhlau, 1883–2009)
WA Br   Luther, Martin. *Luthers Werke: Kritische Gesamtausgabe: Briefwechsel*,
            18 vols. (Weimar: H. Böhlau, 1930–1985).
WA DB   Luther, Martin. *Luthers Werke: Kritische Gesamtausgabe: Deutsche Bibel*,
            12 vols. (Weimar: H. Böhlau, 1906–1961).
WA TR   Luther, Martin. *Luthers Werke: Kritische Gesamtausgabe: Tischreden*,
            6 vols. (Weimar: H. Böhlau, 1912–1921).

Treatise on Good Works

1520

TIMOTHY J. WENGERT

INTRODUCTION[1]

In late March of 1520, one month after he started to prepare for publication a "sermon" on good works, Martin Luther wrote to his contact at the Saxon court, Georg Spalatin (1484–1545): "It will not be a sermon but rather a small book, and if my writing progresses as well as it has, this book will be the best work I have published so far."[a] Although the better-known pamphlets of 1520 were still to appear—*Address to the Christian Nobility*, *The Babylonian Captivity of the Church*, and *The Freedom of a Christian*[b]—the finished *Treatise on Good Works* fulfilled Luther's prediction as one of the clearest and most accessible introductions to Luther's reforming work and theology. Luther's main goal was to commend a new, down-to-earth piety to all Christians. This piety was new, because at its center was a radically different meaning of good works that would transform the way believers practiced their faith. That different meaning, it turned out, was

1. This introduction is a revision of the "Translator's Introduction" by Scott Hendrix, in Martin Luther, *Treatise on Good Works*, trans. Scott Hendrix (Minneapolis: Fortress Press, 2012), 2–11. The translation that follows is also a revision of the work by Hendrix.

---

a   WA Br 2:75 (March 25, 1520).

b   For the *Address* and *Freedom of a Christian*, see below, p. 369 and 467. For the *Babylonian Captivity*, see LW 36:3–126.

easy to misunderstand and required a detailed explanation that Luther offered in this "small book."

Today the term "good works" is often associated with acts of charity in general, but in late medieval theology it designated acts of religious devotion and charity that made up for sins committed by believers and thus were considered meritorious for salvation. Already in the Sermon on the Mount, Jesus said, "Let your light shine before others, so that they may see your good works and give glory to your Father in heaven."[2] Augustine of Hippo (354–430), the bishop and theologian whom Martin Luther cited more than any other, debated with his Pelagian opponents the place of good works in the Christian life.[3] Augustine was the source of Luther's claim that actions that appear to be good works are in fact sinful unless done in faith.[c]

In the *Rule of St. Benedict* (c. 480–542), "good works" are given a primary role in monastic life. Chapter 4, titled "The Instruments of Good Works," concludes with the following admonition: "Behold, these are instruments of the spiritual art, which, if they have been applied without ceasing day and night and approved on judgment day, will merit for us from the Lord that reward which he has promised." These "instruments" of merit are also evident in a definition from a popular medieval dictionary of theology printed in 1517: "Certain works are directed toward our neighbor and pertain to love of neighbor, while others are directed toward God alone and pertain to divine worship and adoration."[d] By the sixteenth century, such good works were a required part of the Christian life that applied to every believer who desired eternal life. Often, these basic religious works were outlined by another part of the Sermon on the Mount, where Jesus talked about prayer, almsgiving, and fasting.

When confronted with Martin Luther's basic message, readers and listeners were sometimes confused or angered

2. Matt. 5:16. The term "good works" also appears in the Vulgate text of 2 Pet. 1:10 and was therefore present in the Latin Bible of the Middle Ages; but the phrase, for which there is only moderate textual evidence, is absent from most English translations of 2 Pet. 1:10.

3. In his later career, Augustine's opponents included the British monk, Pelagius (354–420) and his adherents, who insisted that human beings were born with the ability to resist sin and could thus fulfill God's gracious commandments. These "Pelagians" were condemned in various councils of the ancient church.

---

c   Hans-Ulrich Delius, *Augustin als Quelle Luthers,* 3d ed. (Berlin, 1984), 66.

d   Johannes Altenstaig (d. c. 1525), *Vocabularius theologiae* (Hagenau, 1517), fol. 169b.

by what they read and heard about good works. In sermons and pamphlets, Luther and his colleagues claimed that salvation came by faith alone and not by works. Their assertion was based on their reading of biblical verses like Rom. 3:28, "For we hold that a person is justified by faith apart from works prescribed by the law"; or Eph. 2:8-9, "For by grace you have been saved through faith, and this is not your own doing; it is the gift of God—not the result of works, so that no one may boast." Even though, they argued, Paul's message did not overthrow the law, understood especially as the Ten Commandments, still the origin of Christian good works came from faith.[4]

Some of Luther's readers and listeners charged that his position implied that believers were free from the obligation to perform any good works at all—a complaint to which not only Luther but also other early preachers who defended Luther's views had to respond. One preacher described the opposing attitude this way: "If it is true, all the better, we need to perform no good works; we will gladly take faith alone. And if praying, fasting, holy days, and almsgiving are not required, then we will lie near the stove, warm our feet on its tiles, turn the roasting apples, open our mouths, and wait until grilled doves fly into them."[5]

The late medieval believers who heard that good works would not save them associated those good works with religious activities that were no longer necessary for salvation. The quotation above mentions praying, fasting, worship, and almsgiving, which Luther and his supporters viewed as appropriate works for believers. But the list of unnecessary works included acquiring indulgences, venerating and praying to saints, making pilgrimages to their shrines, holding private Masses (said by a priest without communicants), requiring clerical celibacy, making binding monastic vows, venerating relics, and so on.[6] In the *Treatise on Good Works*, Luther takes pains to distinguish these activities, which he calls the "wrong kind of good works," from the "right kind of good works," namely, those nurturing faith and obeying the Ten Commandments out of faith. For that reason, the treatise shows how faith, by which one is saved, leads

4. See, e.g., Rom. 3:31; 10:4; and Gal. 2:15-21.

5. Urbanus Rhegius (1489–1541), a preacher at Augsburg, *Anzeigung, daß die römische Bulle merklichen Schaden in Gewissen mancher Menschen gebracht und nicht Doctor Luthers Lehre* (Augsburg, 1521), C4r–v. These examples of leisure relate to *Schlaraffenland*, an imaginary place mentioned in European fairy tales that was alleged to contain a surplus of everything. Luther also alludes to it in this *Treatise*, p. 359, n. 126.

6. For an exhaustive list of religious practices Luther regarded as for the most part unnecessary in the "true Christian church," see his *Exhortation to All the Clergy* (1530), written during the Diet of Augsburg (LW 34:54–59).

inevitably to obedience, that is, how properly fulfilling the first commandment ("You shall have no other gods") leads to obedience of the remaining commandments—and all of this not as a human work at all but as a gift and work of the Holy Spirit. This theme appears repeatedly throughout the composition, as if to say: the right kind of good works follow from faith, just as the last nine commandments follow the first. Another significant theme attacks the late medieval distinction between commands and counsels, where lay believers in a state of grace had to fulfill the Ten Commandments but those under a vow and hence in a state of perfection also could also fulfill Jesus' "counsels" of poverty, chastity, and obedience as a higher level of Christian obedience. For Luther, there is enough simply in the Ten Commandments to keep every Christian busy.

Luther preached on the Ten Commandments throughout his career. His *Small Catechism* and *Large Catechism* (1529) remain the best-known expositions of the commandments, but prior to 1529 Luther had preached and written on them six times: 1516–1517, 1518, 1520, 1522, 1525, and 1528. A sermon from 1528 reveals why Luther deemed the Ten Commandments so important—namely, to foster a proper understanding of Christian freedom: "It used to be that the Sabbath was 'made holy' in that after hearing a Mass we spent the day getting drunk. Now, too, we abuse the Sabbath, going in and out of the church by habit to hear a sermon but not observing the word. You go in [to church] and come out no wiser than before, snoring and sleeping in church. But that does not sanctify the Sabbath."[7] In other words, Christian freedom from the law and works does not imply license to abuse that freedom by spurning the fruits of faith.

The *Treatise on Good Works* was written with strong encouragement from Georg Spalatin, secretary and court chaplain to Elector Frederick III of Saxony (1463–1525), to whom, as noted above, Luther enthusiastically reported on his progress. One month before that letter, however, Spalatin had reminded him of a promise to compose a sermon on good works. Luther replied that he did not remember the

7. WA 31/1:66, 29–32. See also LC, "Ten Commandments," par. 96–97, in BC, 399.

promise and, besides, had already published so much that nobody would buy it. Two days later, however, he wrote to Spalatin that he did remember and would get down to work.

It was the beginning of a very busy twelve months. On 9 January 1520, the legal proceedings against Luther were reopened in Rome, and Pope Leo X (1475–1521) had appointed three commissions to prepare a denunciation of the German professor. In June, the denunciation was issued in the form of a papal edict, *Exsurge Domine*, which threatened Luther with excommunication if he did not recant. The papal ban of excommunication itself took effect in January of 1521. Meanwhile, Luther was lecturing on the Psalms and composing one important work after another. His rejection of the pope's claim to be the vicar of Christ and to rule over the entire church appeared in May of 1520 under the title *The Papacy at Rome*.[8]

8. LW 39:49–104.

In the midst of the confrontation between Luther and the papal Curia, this tract on good works appeared. Judging by the number of reprints and editions, it was popular and sold well. The first edition was printed by Melchior Lotter Jr. (c. 1490–1542) in Wittenberg and appeared in late May or early June of 1520. Before the end of the year, the treatise had been reprinted eight times, with another six reprints appearing in 1521. That same year, a Latin translation was published in Leipzig and then reprinted in Wittenberg. It was followed by translations into other languages: English, French, Dutch, and Low German, a dialect spoken in the lowlands of northern Germany.

Some refer to the treatise as the *Sermon on Good Works*, presumably because it started as a sermon and because the title of at least one edition claimed that it had been preached. The title of the first edition, however, is simply *Von den guten Werken*, best rendered in English as *Good Works* or literally as *Concerning Good Works*. As Luther said, however, it turned out to be a small book, and therefore this edition uses the title *Treatise*, as did the American edition of Luther's works.

Luther argues that the Ten Commandments define all the good works for the Christian life. The first commandment is fulfilled through faith, which is the first and chief

Von den guten Wercken: D.M. L

Wittenberg.

This historiated title page border of Luther's *Treatise on Good Works* features the crest of the printer, Melchior Lotter the Younger, at the foot. It has been attributed to Lucas Cranach the Elder or to his workshop.

good work that leads to and undergirds all the others. Reflecting a late medieval approach to good works that emphasized Christian virtues, Luther defines the kind of good work proceeding from that faith for each commandment. Thus, the second commandment is fulfilled by praise (of God and thus not of the self), the third by worship (understood as attending Mass, hearing preaching, and prayer [especially corporate prayer]), the fourth by obedience to superiors and solicitude to underlings, the fifth by gentleness, the sixth by purity and chastity, the seventh by generosity, and the eighth by truth telling.[9] Additionally, when Luther is ready to explain the second commandment against taking God's name in vain, he does it under the heading of "the second good work." He then discusses the ways through which the second commandment is obeyed, and he identifies four of those ways, each of which he calls a work of the second commandment. In this case, the term "good work" refers both collectively to obeying the second commandment and specifically to the ways in which that obedience can take place. His explanations of the third and fourth commandments are also extensive, but after that Luther, perhaps realizing that his sermon had indeed become a book, devotes less space to the last six commandments. His commentary on the last two commandments is compressed into one paragraph.

The headings under which the work or works of each commandment are explained are not uniform. At the fourth commandment, the traditional division of the commandments into two tables leads Luther to call the fourth commandment "the first commandment of the second table

9. Unlike the later Reformed penchant for numbering the commandments according to the Hebrew text (and thus adding a second commandment against images), Luther follows the tradition of the Greek and Latin texts by dividing the commandments

of Moses." As in many of Luther's early writings, the paragraphs are numbered consecutively throughout the entire treatise, a customary way of dividing late medieval tracts and sermons. Here Luther numbers the paragraphs consecutively through the first two commandments, but after that the numbering of paragraphs starts over within each commandment. His explanations of the first four commandments are much longer than those of the last six, and his treatment of prayer, which is the third work of the third commandment, is a little treatise in itself.

Biblical passages are translated as Luther cited or phrased them rather than according to modern translations. At this point in Luther's career, there was no standard German translation of the Bible (Luther's German New Testament appeared first in 1522). As was common among late medieval preachers, Luther had in mind or sometimes even cited a text in Latin and rendered it into German as a paraphrased translation. Thus, although his citations may not appear to today's readers as accurate, they are in fact a blend of citation and explanation not at all unusual for his day. Luther's biblical citations arise from the Vulgate, or Latin version of the Bible, much of which he knew by heart.

On the advice of Spalatin, Luther dedicated the treatise to Duke John (1486–1532), the brother of Luther's first prince, Elector Frederick III of Saxony. In 1525, Elector Frederick died, and Duke John became the new elector. John was firmly committed to Luther and his colleagues and did all he could to ensure the survival of Wittenberg theology and practice in Saxony and beyond. Besides leading the Saxon delegation at the Diet of Augsburg and signing the *Augsburg Confession* (1530), Elector John led the reform of the University of Wittenberg and endorsed the inspection and reorganization of parishes (starting in 1527), in which the evangelical forms of worship and piety recommended by Luther were often utilized. Although Luther could not have foreseen it in 1520, he could not have dedicated a more fitting piece to Duke John than the *Treatise on Good Works*.

The translation of the treatise is based primarily on the text in Luther's German edited by Hans-Ulrich Delius and

to covet into two, and h‹
prohibition of images as
expansion of the first commandment ‹‹.
the Israelites.

Duke John of Saxony.
Portrait by Lucas Cranach
the Elder, 1534.

Rudolf Mau in *Martin Luther Studienausgabe*, with constant reference to the critical "Weimar" edition of Luther's works.[e] That text is taken from the first printed edition that came from the press of Melchior Lotter Jr. in Wittenberg around the end of May 1520. The editors also took into consideration the text of Luther's manuscript that was discovered in 1892. A comparison of the printed edition with the manuscript reveals a number of variations and alterations, some of which come from the printer. In addition, other modern versions have been consulted.[f]

TREATISE ON GOOD WORKS[10]

JESUS.[11]

TO THE ILLUSTRIOUS AND NOBLE prince and lord, John, Duke of Saxony, Landgrave of Thuringia, Margrave of Meissen, my gracious lord and patron.

Illustrious and noble prince, gracious lord, with my humble prayer I am always at the service of your princely majesty.

10. See the final paragraph of the introduction.

11. Following a monastic tradition, Luther began many of his early writings and letters with this word.

e   *Martin Luther Studienausgabe*, vol. 2, ed. Hans-Ulrich Delius (Berlin: Evangelische Verlagsanstalt, 1982), 12–88; and WA 6:196–276. The manuscript in Luther's hand is found in WA 9:226–301.

f   *Die guten Werke*, in *Martin Luther Taschenausgabe*, vol. 4, *Evangelium und Leben*, ed. Horst Beintker (Berlin: Evangelische Verlagsanstalt, 1983), 36–131; *Von den guten Werken*, ed. Werner Jetter, in *Martin Luther Ausgewählte Schriften*, vol. 1: *Aufbruch zur Reformation*, ed. Karin Bornkamm and Gerhard Ebeling, 2d ed. (Frankfurt am Main: Insel, 1983), 38–149.

Gracious prince and lord. For some time I have wanted to acknowledge my humble devotion and duty to your grace with one of the spiritual wares that suit my position, but I found myself unfit for the task of creating a gift that would be worthy of you. Now, however, my most gracious Lord Frederick, Duke of Saxony, Elector of the Holy Roman Empire, Vicar, etc.,[12] and brother of your princely grace, has not disdained to receive my amateurish little book, which was dedicated to him and now much to my surprise has been published.[13] I am encouraged by his gracious example and make bold to presume that, just as both of you have the same noble blood, you also have the same noble spirit evident in a mild and beneficent disposition. I hope, therefore, that your princely grace will not scorn my poor, humble offering, which I have found more necessary to publish than any of my other sermons or pamphlets, because good works, which involve much greater deception and cunning than anything else, have provoked the most controversy. In this matter, it is easy to take advantage of ordinary people, and for that reason our Lord Christ commanded us to beware of sheep's clothing that hides the wolf underneath.[g] Good works have more things added to and subtracted from them than any gold, silver, precious stones, or other expensive things, even though such works must have the same, simple goodness; otherwise, they are mere fakes that sparkle with pretty colors.

I know full well and hear daily that many people belittle my poverty and say I produce only little pamphlets and sermons in German for the uneducated laity. That does not bother me, however. Would God that I had worked my whole life and devoted all my ability to the improvement of one layperson! I would be satisfied with this, give thanks to God, and willingly let all my little books turn to dust. I will let others judge whether or not writing many thick books is a scholarly method that serves Christendom well; but if I wanted to write big books in their way, I think I could produce them faster than they could prepare a small sermon in

12. Following courtly protocol, Luther lists Elector Frederick's chief offices. "Vicar," a position in the political hierarchy of the Holy Roman Empire (the official surrogate for the emperor when he was absent, was held by Duke John's brother, Elector Frederick, who was Luther's overlord. After Frederick's death in 1525, his brother, John, to whom Luther is dedicating this writing, succeeded him as elector.

13. *Fourteen Consolations for Those Who Labor and Are Heavy-Laden*, written for and dedicated to the ailing Elector Frederick in August 1519 (LW 42:117–66; WA 6:99–134). Georg Spalatin produced a German translation that was made from Luther's Latin manuscript, and both versions were published at Wittenberg in February of 1520, the same month that Spalatin reminded Luther of a promise to write a treatise on good works.

g   An allusion to Matt. 7:15.

my way. If reaching a goal were as easy as pursuing it, then Christ would long since have been thrown out of heaven and the throne of God overturned. "Even though we cannot all be authors, we want to be critics all the same."[h] I will happily let others have the honor of great accomplishments and will not be ashamed to preach and write in German for the uneducated laity. Although I can only do a little, I am of the mind that Christendom would have benefited much more from such activities (had we occupied ourselves with it sooner and tried to keep it up) than from the learned tomes and disputations conducted only by scholars at the universities. Moreover, I have never forced or invited anyone to listen to me or read my sermons. I have openly and dutifully served the community[i] with what God has given me, and whoever is not pleased can read and listen to someone else. Nor does it bother me if my contribution is not needed. For me it is more than enough that a few of the laity, especially the most eminent of them, deign to read my sermons.

Even if other incentives were lacking, I have plenty now that I have learned how much your princely grace has been pleased by these German pamphlets and desires to know more about good works and faith. It has pleased me to provide this service as diligently as I can, and as your humble subject I request your princely grace kindly to accept this opus of mine until God grants me time to offer a full explanation of faith. For now I wanted to indicate how we should practice and use faith in every good work and allow it to be the noblest work of all. If God permits, at another time I will treat the [Apostles'] Creed and how we should daily pray and recite it.[j] Herewith I commend myself humbly to your princely grace.

---

h   A rhymed German adage also found in the Latin. See Wander, 1:582.

i   *Gemeinde*: his Wittenberg congregation and community.

j   German: *den Glauben* (the faith). Luther published an explanation of the Apostles' Creed in 1520 along with explanations of the Ten Commandments and the Lord's Prayer that had been printed in 1518 and 1519 (WA 7:194–229).

Wittenberg, the twenty-ninth day of March, one thousand five hundred and twenty years after the birth of Christ.

Your princely grace's obedient chaplain, Doctor Martin Luther, Augustinian at Wittenberg.

[Introduction]

1. It should be known, first of all, that no good works exist other than those that God has commanded, just as there is no sin other than what God has forbidden. Whoever wishes to recognize and perform good works need only learn God's commandments.[14] Accordingly, Christ says in Matt. 19[:17]: "If you wish to enter life, keep the commandments." And when the young man asks in Matt. 19[:16-19] what he has to do to be saved, Christ holds up to him the Ten Commandments and nothing else. Therefore we must learn to distinguish among good works from God's commandments and not from the appearance, magnitude, or quantity of the deeds themselves or from human opinion, laws, or approaches. We have seen how this happened in the past and still happens owing to our blindness and complete disdain for God's commandments.

14. Luther is setting up a contrast between the God-given Ten Commandments, on the one hand, and human regulations and Christ's so-called counsels, on the other.

[The First Good Work]*k*

2. The foremost and noblest good work is faith in Christ, just as he himself said in John 6[:28-29] when the Jews asked him what they should do in order to perform good works of God. He answered: "This is the (good) work of God, that you believe in him whom he has sent." Now when we hear this or preach it, we pass right over it, thinking it is a small thing that is easy to do. We should instead pause here a long time and ponder it in depth. For all good works have to be

k Luther relates this first good work, faith, to the first commandment, beginning below in par. 9 (p. 274).

15. A reference to the medieval practice of a lesser noble receiving a grant of land from his lord, so that the former must live totally from the benevolence of the latter. So all good works arise out of faith.

16. Luther investigates a first aspect of faith: its relation to works.

17. Luther refers here to medieval Scholastic theologians who insisted believers could not be certain whether they were in a state of grace, where they would receive due reward for their good works. See Luther's encounter with Cardinal Cajetan (1469–1534) in 1518, above, pp. 141–47.

18. See Matt. 6:1-18, used in the Middle Ages to define three categories of good works. This begins Luther's discussion of the first level of faith.

included in this one and receive their goodness from it, as if receiving a fief.[15] We have to make it simple and clear so that it can be understood.[16] We find that many people pray, fast, create pious endowments, do this and that, and lead respectable lives in the opinion of others; but if you ask them whether or not they are certain that God is pleased with what they do, they do not know or at least have their doubts. Moreover, they cite learned scholars who do nothing but teach good works and claim it is unnecessary to have such certainty.[17] See here! All these good works are performed apart from faith; they amount to nothing and are completely dead, because the attitude of your conscience before God determines the goodness of the works that proceed from it. If there is no faith or good conscience toward God, your works are decapitated, and your life and goodness amount to nothing at all. Now you see why, whenever I exalt faith and reject as false those works done without it, they accuse me of forbidding good works, although my real desire is to teach the genuine good works that belong to faith.[*I*]

3. If you then ask these people the following: when they are on the job, walking or standing still, eating, drinking, sleeping, or engaging in any activity that sustains the body or promotes the common good, do they consider their actions to be good works pleasing to God? You will find they say no. They define good works very narrowly and confine them to church-related activities like praying, fasting, and giving alms.[18] The rest are done in vain, people think, and lack significance in the eyes of God. Thus, their contemptible unbelief causes them to minimize and trivialize the service of God, who on the contrary is served by everything, whatever it may be, that is done, spoken, or conceived in faith. Eccl. 9[:7-9] teaches the same: "Go forth with joy, eat and drink, knowing that your work pleases God. Always clothe yourself in white and keep your head anointed with oil. Spend your

---

I   See charges 31 and 32 in the papal bull, *Exsurge Domini*, published in October 1520. For a later example of this same charge, see the *Augsburg Confession* XX.1–2 in BC, 52–53.

life with the wife you love all the days of these uncertain times that are granted to you."[19] For our clothing *always* to be white means that without distinction all our works are good, no matter what we call them. They are white when I am certain and believe that they please God; then the head of my soul will never lack the oil of a good conscience. Therefore Christ says in John 8[:29], "I always do what is pleasing to him." How could it have been "always" unless it included those times when he was eating, drinking, and sleeping? And St. John says in 1 John 3[:19-22]: "By this we know that we stand in the truth, when we can comfort our hearts and have confidence in his presence. Even if our heart afflicts us with remorse, God is greater than our heart . . . and we have assurance . . . that we will receive that which we have sought because we keep his commandments and do what pleases him."*m* Again [1 John 3:9]: "Those who have been born of God" (that is, believe and trust God) "do not sin . . . (and) cannot sin." And Ps. 34[:22]: "None of those who trust in him shall sin." And Ps. 2[:11]: "Blessed are those who trust in him."*n* If this is true, then everything they do must be good, or the evil they do must be quickly forgiven. Now do you see why I exalt faith so highly and gather all works within it and reject all works that do not flow from faith?

4. All individuals*o* are able to tell and feel whether or not what they do is good. If their hearts are confident that their work is pleasing to God, then it is good even if it were something as trivial as picking up a straw. If the heart is unsure instead of confident, then the work is not good even if it raised all the dead and the doers gave their bodies to be burned.*p* Paul teaches that very thing in Rom. 14[:23]: "For whatever does not proceed from faith is sin." We are called believers in Christ only on the basis of faith as the chief work and not on the basis of other works, which can also be done

19. Luther's rendering of Eccl. 9:7-9. In his commentary on the Bible, Nicholas of Lyra (c. 1270–1349) associated white clothing with a holy life but the oil with divine grace. Following the general pattern of biblical translation before his own translation of 1522, Luther renders texts freely according to the Latin Vulgate. See the editor's introduction above, p. 263.

---

m   Luther's rendering of the text.

n   In both psalms, Luther renders the Vulgate's "hope" (NRSV: "take refuge") with "trust."

o   Singular in the original.

p   See 1 Cor. 13:3.

20. Luther's term for adherents of Islam, who were familiar to sixteenth-century Europeans primarily as Muslims from the Ottoman Turkish Empire.

21. Luther attacks the cornerstone of late medieval, Aristotelian ethics, that a person becomes good by doing good and that faith, hope, and love are simply (theological) virtues. See *The Freedom of a Christian* below, p. 487.

22. For medieval theologians, the term *habitus* referred to a disposition infused in the soul, created by grace, and containing the virtues faith, hope, and love. Luther objected to this concept because *habitus* was not a biblical term and because it emphasized faith as a static quality of the soul instead of trust in God.

by pagans, Jews, Turks,[20] and sinners. Firm trust, however, that God is pleased with them is possible only for Christians enlightened and fortified by grace.

The reason that speaking this way seems strange and I have been called a heretic comes about because these people adhere to blind reason and pagan ways of thinking and have not set faith above other virtues but on the same level with them and assigned to faith its own work, which is then isolated from the works of other virtues.[21] Faith alone, however, validates all other works and makes them acceptable and worthy, as long as the doers trust God and do not doubt that God approves everything they do. Those who criticize me, however, have not allowed faith to remain a work but have made of it a *habitus*,[22] although nowhere does Scripture call anything a divine good work except faith alone.[q] No wonder, then, that they are blind and have become leaders of the blind.[r] This faith [of which I speak] is soon joined by love, peace, joy,[s] and hope. To those who trust God, God immediately gives the Holy Spirit, as St. Paul tells the Galatians [Gal. 3:2]: "You have received the Spirit not because of your good works but because you have believed God's word."[t]

5. In this faith all works become equal. One is like the other, and all distinctions among them disappear whether they are large or small, short or long [in duration], many or few. Works are pleasing not for their own sake but because of faith, which is present in one and the same way in every work. That faith is alive and efficacious no matter how different the works are from one another, just as our bodily members derive their life, functions, and names from the head and without the head would have none of those. Moreover, it follows that a Christian who lives in this faith does

q   John 6:29. For Luther, faith is a work that God effects in human beings.

r   A reference by Jesus to the Pharisees in Matt. 15:14.

s   Love, peace, and joy are named fruits of the Spirit in Gal. 5:22.

t   Citing the text as a statement, not a question.

not need to be taught good works and instead does whatever is there to be done. And it is well done, as St. Samuel[u] said to Saul [1 Sam. 10:6-7]: "[When] the Spirit . . . will possess you, you will . . . be turned into a different person, and . . . do whatever you see fit to do, for God is with you." Thus, we also read about St. Hannah, Samuel's mother, that when she believed the priest Eli, who assured her of God's grace, she went home happy and content, and from that time on she no longer wandered around from place to place. That is, whatever happened was all the same to her.[v] St. Paul Paul also says [2 Cor. 3:17]: "Where the Spirit of Christ is, everything is free."[w] Faith does not allow itself to be bound to any work nor to be deprived of any work. Instead, as Ps. 1[:3] says: They "yield their fruit in its time," that is, as the time comes and goes.

6. We may illustrate this with a common, down-to-earth example. When a husband or wife cherishes and pleases the other spouse and truly believes it, who needs to teach them how to act or what to do, when to speak or not, or what to think about the other? Their own confidence alone teaches all that and more. There is no difference in the works they do, be they great or small, extended or brief, many or few. They do them all with joyful, serene, and confident hearts and are completely free.[x] But if uncertainty is present, they look for the best thing to do and thus begin imagining there to be differences among the works by which they may gain the other's affection. Then they must walk around with heavy hearts and with no enthusiasm, completely trapped, half despairing, and as often as not they end up acting the fool.

---

u   Luther, like most in his day, regarded the patriarchs, prophets, and other faithful women and men of Hebrew Scripture as saints.

v   1 Sam. 1:6-28, esp. vv. 18-19.

w   The NRSV, following the Greek and Latin, has "Spirit of the Lord."

x   Literally: "a completely free journeyman," a saying derived from the guilds and the "graduation" from apprentice to journeyman. An English equivalent might be "As free as the wind."

23. Here and elsewhere, Luther attacks a cornerstone of late medieval piety and theology, that a person must always doubt his or her standing before God, not knowing for certain whether one's sorrow for sin or subsequent good works truly please God. This humility of uncertainty was seen as an especially important good, meritorious work over against the sin of pride.

24. The burial shrine of St. James at Santiago de Compostela in northwestern Spain was a favorite destination for pilgrims.

25. Luther later recalled that he visited some of the holy places in Rome during his sojourn in late 1511 and early 1512.

26. The trip to Rome has been convincingly redated (from 1510 to 1511) by Hans Schneider, "Martin Luthers Reise nach Rom neu datiert und neu gedeutet," in *Studien zur Wissenschafts- und Religionsgeschichte*, ed. Akademie der Wissenschaften zu Göttingen (Berlin: De Gruyter, 2011), 1–157.

27. Special prayers ascribed to Bridget (Birgitta), a Swedish saint who died in Rome in 1373, were popular among late medieval Christians.

28. Luther introduces a second aspect of faith.

Individual Christians,[y] therefore, who live with this confidence in God, know all things,[z] are able to do all things, take responsibility for all that needs to be done, and do it all joyfully and freely, not in order to accumulate merits and works but in order to fulfill their desire to please God in this way, to serve God simply without return, being satisfied that God is pleased. On the other hand, those who are not one with God or uncertain about it begin to look anxiously for ways to make satisfaction and sway God with many works.[23] They run to St. James,[24] Rome,[25, 26] Jerusalem, here or there, pray to St. Bridget (d. 1373) to grant this or that,[27] fast on this or that day, make confession here, make confession there, beseech this or that person, and yet they find no rest. And they do all this with such great heaviness, doubts, and lack of enthusiasm in their hearts that Hebrew Scripture calls such good works *aven amal*, in German "toil and trouble."[a] They are not good works at all but a complete waste. This matter has driven many people mad and made them miserable with anxiety. The Wisd. of Sol. 5[:6-7] states about them: "We have worn ourselves out on unrighteous paths and we have taken ways that are arduous and bitter; we have not known the way of God and the sun of righteousness has not risen over us."[b]

7. Given that in such works, faith is still paltry and weak, let us inquire further about cases when people suffer with respect to their body, property, reputation, friends, or anything else.[28] Do they then believe they are still pleasing to God and—be their suffering and adversity great or small—that God is still mercifully disposed toward them? In this situation, when all our senses and understanding tell us that God is angry, it is an art to trust in God and to regard oneself as better cared for than it appears. In this situation,

y   Singular in the original.

z   Cf. 1 Cor. 2:15-16.

a   Ps. 90:10. But see also Job 4:8; 5:6; Pss. 10:7; 55:11; Isa. 10:1.

b   A close paraphrase of Wisd. of Sol. 5:6-7. Throughout his career, Luther cited passages from the Apocrypha, to which he later accorded a secondary authority but also included in his translation of the complete Bible in 1534.

God is hidden,[c] just as the bride says in the Song of Sol. [2:9]: "Look, there he stands behind our wall gazing in at the windows."[29] That is: during our sufferings, which try to separate us from God like a wall or even a barrier, he stands there hidden and yet sees me and does not leave me. He is standing ready to help with grace and allows himself to be seen through the window of a dim faith. In Lam. [3:31-33, paraphrased], Jeremiah says: "God rejects mortals but never with callous disregard." They have no experience with this kind of faith but instead give up, thinking that God has abandoned them and become their enemy. They attribute their affliction to other people and the devil, and there is no trust in God whatsoever. For this reason, they forever view their suffering as offensive and harmful, and then they go out and do what they think are good works without recognizing any lack of faith on their part. But those who in the midst of such suffering trust in God and are completely confident that God is pleased with them consider their suffering and adversity to be nothing but costly merits and precious assets, the value of which no one can appreciate. For faith and confidence render precious before God everything that to others is the worst that can happen. That applies even to dying, according to Ps. 116[:15]: "The death of the saints is considered precious in the eyes of God." As much as confidence and faith are greater and stronger at this level than they are when there is no suffering, so also the afflictions that are endured in faith are likewise superior to any and all works done in faith. In this way, suffering produces immeasurably greater advantages than such works can ever provide.

8. Above these is the highest level of faith of all,[30] which is required when God torments the conscience not with earthly afflictions but with death, hell, and sin and withholds divine grace and mercy, as if God wanted to condemn and stay angry forever, something that only a few people experience, as David laments in Ps. 6[:1]: "Do not ... discipline me in your wrath."[31] To trust that God is gracious

29. Luther, like many other interpreters before him, applied the Song of Solomon to the relation of the believer and Christ.

30. Luther's third aspect of faith.

31. This idea is similar to the medieval *resignatio ad infernum*. For an earlier example, see Luther's *Lectures on Romans* (1515-1516), in LW 25:379-84.

c   This argument is closely related to Luther's theology of the cross. See the *Heidelberg Disputation*, above, pp. 98-101.

in this situation is the finest work that can occur in and through any creature. The "work saints" and "doers of good deeds" know nothing about this; for how could they be certain of God's goodness and grace, since they are not certain regarding their own works and have doubts about even the lowest level of faith?

Now you can see why I have insisted that faith should always be praised and that every work done without faith should be rejected: to lead the people away from the false, hypocritical, pharisaical, faithless good works that now fill to overflowing the cloisters, churches, houses, and all levels of society, and to direct them toward the true, genuinely good and faithful works. No one contradicts me except the unclean animals with uncloven hooves, as Moses says in the law,*d* who cannot stand to make any distinction among good works. Instead, they fall into the trap of thinking that when they have prayed, fasted, endowed Masses, and made confession and satisfaction,*e* everything will be well with them, even though they are not confident of receiving divine grace and blessing. For the most part, they consider it good when they have performed many great things over a long period without such confidence and only then expect good things for themselves after the works are done. Thus, they count on them instead of on God's goodwill; that is, they build on sand and water and must suffer a horrible collapse, as Christ says in Matt. 7[:26-27]. On Christmas night, the angels proclaimed this kindness and goodwill from heaven when they sang: "*Gloria in excelsis Deo.* Glory to God in the highest, peace on earth and goodwill to all people."*f*

9. Do you see? This is the work of the first commandment: "You shall not have other gods."[32] That is to say: Since I alone am God, all your confidence, trust, and faith should be placed only in me and no one else. You do not "have a

32. Following these introductory paragraphs about faith and its three aspects (fruits, suffering, and resignation), Luther now turns to an exposition of the first commandment (Exod. 20:3; Deut. 5:7). Luther associates this commandment with faith throughout his career. See, e.g., LC, "Ten Commandments," par. 1–4 (BC, 386).

d Cf. Lev. 11:1-8. An indirect, sarcastic use of allegory to refer to those who in fact disagreed with his view of good works.

e Two parts of the sacrament of penance.

f Luke 2:14. Luther is citing a translation of the Greek reflected in the Vulgate and the Latin Mass and used in sixteenth-century German and English translations.

god" when all you do is mouth the word or worship by bowing the knee or making external gestures instead of trusting God from the heart and counting on God's goodness, grace, and favor in all that you do or suffer, in living and dying, in weal and in woe, just as Christ said to the Samaritan woman in John 4[:24]: "I say to you, whoever worships God must worship in spirit and truth." And this faith, trust, and confidence, which come from the bottom of the heart, are the true fulfillment of the first commandment. Without them no work of any kind can satisfy its demand. Just as this commandment is the first, highest, and best, from which and to which all the others flow and by which they are evaluated and judged, so also the work that fulfills it (trust and confidence in God's favor at all times) is the first, noblest, and best work from which and to which all the others flow, in which they abide and by which they must be judged and evaluated. To do other works against this one is to act as if neither the first commandment nor God existed. Hence St. Augustine rightly calls the work that fulfills the first commandment faith, hope, and love.[g] It was said above that such confidence and faith bring with them love and hope. In fact, rightly considered, love should be first or at least on the same level with faith. For I cannot trust God without believing that he is favorably inclined toward me. As a consequence, I am favorably inclined toward God and moved to trust him from the heart and rely on him for everything good.

10. Now consider all those who do not trust God all the time nor expect divine favor and benevolence in all their working or suffering, living or dying, but instead look for those things elsewhere or from themselves. They do not keep this commandment and are in fact practicing idolatry even though they were to perform the works of all the other commandments and, in addition, pile up prayer to all the saints along with fasting, obedience, patience, chastity, and innocence. The chief work is not there, without which all the

---

g   "God is to be worshiped with faith, hope, and love." Augustine, *Enchiridion* 1, 3 in *Basic Writings of Saint Augustine*, ed. Whitney J. Oates (New York: Random House, 1948), 1:658 [= MPL 40:232].

others are nothing but pure glitter, show, and makeup with nothing underneath. Christ warns us against this in Matt. 7[:15]: "Beware of false prophets who come to you in sheep's clothing." That means all those who try to make themselves pleasing to God through many good works (as they call them) and buy God's favor as if God were a peddler or a day laborer, who did not want to give away his grace and favor for nothing. Such characters are the most perverse people on earth; they can never or only with great difficulty be turned in the right direction. Others act like them when in adversity they run to and fro seeking counsel, help, and consolation from everyone and everything except God, from whom they are strictly commanded to request it. The prophet Isaiah in chapter 9[:13] chastises these people in this way: "The unwise folk do not turn to him who strikes them." God struck them by sending them suffering and adversity so that they would seek and trust God, but they ran away instead to other people, sometimes in Egypt, sometimes in Assyria, and even to the devil. That idolatry is recorded by the same prophet and in the books of Kings.*h* All holy hypocrites act the same way: when something bad happens, instead of running to God they flee away in fear, wondering how they can get rid of their troubles either by themselves or with others' help and yet be regarded by themselves and others as godly.

11. In many places, St. Paul holds this opinion and attributes so much to faith that he writes [Rom. 1:17], "*Justus ex fide sua vivit*," that is (in German), that "righteous persons have life from their faith" and that "on account of faith they are accounted righteous before God."[33] If righteousness consists in faith, it is clear that faith alone fulfills all the commandments and makes all their works righteous, especially since nobody is just unless all the commandments are kept and, contrariwise, that no works are able to justify in God's sight apart from faith. Moreover, the holy apostle rejects works and praises faith so completely that some people have taken umbrage at his words and said: "Then we will do no

33. Rom. 1:17; 3:28. Following the typical pattern of late medieval preachers, Luther first cites the Latin of Rom. 1:17 and provides a translation, but then adds Rom. 3:28. Singular in the original.

h   See, e.g., 1 Kgs. 36:1-30 or Isaiah 36.

more good works." He condemns such people as mistaken and simpleminded.[i]

Nevertheless, the same thing is still going on now. Whenever we reject impressive, showy works done without faith today, people say that they should only believe and do nothing good at all—as if the first commandment were to be obeyed now by singing, reading, playing the organ, saying Mass, and praying at Matins, Vespers and other appointed times, by endowing churches, altars and cloisters and adorning them with bells, expensive ornaments, vestments, and altar ware, and even by collecting treasures[34] or running to Rome or to the shrines of the saints. If that were true, then, whenever we don our vestments and bow, genuflect, pray the rosary and the Psalms, and do all that not before an idol but before the holy cross of God or a picture of his saints, that is what we would call honoring and worshiping God and, according to the first commandment, having no other gods. Any usurer, adulterer, or sinner of any kind could do that every day. So it is, but if we do these things with the kind of faith that we hold pleases God, then they are praiseworthy not for the sake of their virtuous quality but because of this very faith that makes all works equal, as has been said. If we doubt this, however, or do not believe that God is gracious to us and takes pleasure in us, or measure ourselves to be God pleasing only according to our works, then it is pure deception to honor God externally but internally to elevate ourselves as an idol. That is why I so often have spoken out against and

34. Treasures: perhaps a reference to collections of relics.

Page from the *Heiligthumsbuch*, illustrated by Lucas Cranach and published in 1518, describing the relics from the Castle Church, Wittenberg. The caption reads: "[This reliquary contains] 4 pieces of the mount from which sermon on the mount was delivered; 3 from where Jesus prayed; 2 from where he taught the Lord's Prayer; a stone Jesus stood on in Jerusalem; a piece of the middle of the world; a stone where he wept over Jerusalem; a stone from where Jesus got on the donkey; 2 pieces of the earth where Jesus was arrested. In total: 14 [15] particles."

i   See Rom. 6:1-19. Luther picks up this theme in *The Freedom of a Christian* (below, p. 518).

denounced such works, pomp, and lavishness: so that it is clear as day how they not only take place in doubt or without such faith but also that there is scarcely one person in a thousand who does not set faith in such things, presuming that works make them acceptable to God and eligible for grace. They even make a business of it. God, who has freely promised favor, cannot abide this and instead wants people to begin to rely on his favor and through it accomplish all works whatever their names.

12. From this, note the gap between fulfilling the first commandment only with external works and fulfilling it with innermost trust. The latter makes genuine and living children of God, while the former produces a ruinous idolatry and the most harmful hypocrites on earth. With their pretentious displays, they lead countless people astray, keep them from faith, and leave them woefully seduced, in external mirages and specters. Christ warns us in Matt. 24[:23] about these hypocrites: "Beware of those who say to you, 'Here is the Christ or there he is.'" And in John 4:[21, 23]: "I tell you the time will come that you will worship God neither on this mountain nor in Jerusalem . . ., for the Father seeks those who worship spiritually."

These verses and others like them have caused me and should cause everyone to reject that pompous display of bulls, seals, and banners surrounding indulgences,[35] with which the poor folk are enticed to build churches, make contributions, set up endowments, and offer prayers, even as faith is passed over in silence or, better said, completely suppressed. Since faith makes no distinction among works, it cannot tolerate that some are grossly exaggerated and touted over others but desires only genuine worship and refuses to place that honor or name on any other works unless faith itself imparts it to them. Faith does this so that each work arises in and from faith. This type of mischief is foreshadowed in the Old Testament where the Jews abandon the temple and offer sacrifices in other places, like pleasure gardens and on the mountaintops.*j* Our hypocrites act the same way: eager to perform every work while ignoring the chief work of faith completely.

35. For a description of the ceremonies surrounding indulgences and Luther's criticism in the *95 Theses*, see above, p. 18f.

A typical papal bull, this one by Pope Gregory XIII, who concedes
to the Compagnia di San Paolo the authority to operate a "Monte di Pietà,"
a pawnshop giving charitable loans to the poor, March 1, 1579.

13. Where now are those who ask which works are good,
or what they should do, or how they can become righteous?[k]
Moreover, where are those who, when we preach about faith,
accuse us of denying that any good work should be taught
or done?[l] Is it not true that the first commandment by itself

j   See, e.g., 1 Kgs. 13:33 and Isa. 65:3-7. Luther interprets these events
    typologically.

k   In Luther's German the word *fromm*, which now means "godly" or
    "pious," meant "upright" and was a synonym for *gerecht* (righteous).

l   In the manuscript version of this tract's introduction, Luther points
    to this charge as the basis for writing. See WA 9:229, n. 1.

demands more than anybody can do? Even if a single person became a thousand people or all people or every living creature, there would be enough demanded and more than enough, since it commands each person at every moment to conduct one's life with faith and confidence in God at all times, putting such trust in nothing else, and hence to have no other god than the one true God.

Since, therefore, human nature requires us at every moment to be active or passive, suffering something or fleeing from it (for life never rests, as we see), so then begin here. Let those[m] who desire to be upright and to abound in good works practice faith always, in every situation of life and in all works; let them learn constantly to do or avoid everything in that trust. Then they will discover how much there is to accomplish, how everything is comprehended in faith, and how you can never be idle, because even idleness occurs within the practice and work of faith. In short, when we believe, as we should, that everything that is or happens in us or to us pleases God, then it has to be good and meritorious. Therefore St. Paul says: "So, brothers [and sisters], whether you eat or drink or whatever you do, do everything" "in the name of Jesus Christ our Lord."[n] Now it cannot happen in his name if it does not happen in faith. Rom. 8[:28]: "We know, however, that all things work together for the best for God's holy ones."

When some people say that good works are forbidden when we preach faith alone, it is similar to this. Supposed I advised a sick person: "If you were healthy, your body could perform all its functions, but without your health everything you do is nothing," and someone upon hearing this concluded that I had forbidden the sick man's body to perform any of its functions, even though what I meant was that health had to be there first, which could then stimulate the actions of all the bodily members. Likewise, in all works, faith must be the master artisan[o] and the captain, or they amount to nothing at all.

---

m   Singular in the original.

n   1 Cor. 10:31 with Col. 3:17.

14. Now you might respond: If, through the first commandment, faith does everything, why are there so many ecclesiastical and secular laws, along with rituals in the churches, cloisters, and shrines, which urge and encourage people to do good works?[36] The answer: Precisely because not all of us have faith or pay attention to it. If everyone had it, we would need no law at all, for everyone would perform good works spontaneously all the time, just as such trust would certainly teach them.[37]

Now there are four kinds of people. The first sort (just mentioned) need no law. Paul refers to them in 1 Tim. 1[:9] when he says "the law is not laid down for the righteous person (that is, to the one who has faith), for they do voluntarily what they know and what pleases them, as long as they do it alone with firm trust that in all they do God's good pleasure and favor hover over them. The second kind intends to abuse this freedom by relying on it improperly and becoming lazy. Saint Peter says about them in 1 Pet. 2[:16]: "You should live as those who are free, but do not use this freedom to cloak your sin," as if he were saying: "The freedom of faith does not give free rein to sin and will not cover it up, but it does allow you to do all kinds of works and to suffer whatever comes your way,[p] so that no one is restricted only to this or that specific work." Thus, Paul also says in Gal. 5[:13]: "Take care that this freedom not become a pretext for you to live according to the flesh." Such people have to be prodded with laws and kept in line by teaching and warnings. The third kind consists of malicious persons who are always thinking of ways to sin. Like wild horses and dogs, they must be restrained by the force of ecclesiastical and civil laws and, if that fails, removed from society by the civil sword, as Paul says in Rom. 13[:3-4]: "Civil authority bears the sword and with it serves God . . . not for the godly but to instill fear in the ungodly." The fourth sort of people, who understand this faith and spiritual life in immature

36. Luther is most likely thinking especially of the commands for fasting, praying, confessing one's sins, and receiving the Supper as well as the encouragements to go on pilgrimages, support the poor and the mendicant friars, pray the rosary, and the like.

37. See Luther's exposition of this theme in *The Freedom of a Christian*, below, p. 512.

---

o   German: *Werkmeister*, that is, the guild master who oversees the work of apprentices.

p   Literally: "as they come before your hands." See Eccl. 9:10a.

and childlike ways, have to be enticed and lured like young children with rituals, rules, and external things—readings, praying, fasting, singing, going to church and adorning them, playing organ music, and whatever else is observed in cloisters and churches—until they, too, learn to acknowledge faith. To be sure, a great danger lurks here when—as is happening now—the leaders so emphasize and hammer away at these very rituals and external matters as if they were the true works while ignoring faith. For they should be teaching both things just as a mother gives her children other food along with milk until finally the children can eat solid food by themselves.

15. Because we are not all the same, we must have patience with those people and take upon ourselves and observe what they take upon themselves and observe.[38] We should not despise them but direct them in the proper path of faith. Saint Paul teaches as much in Rom. 14[:1]: "Receive the weak in faith and instruct them." And he did that himself in 1 Cor. 9[:20]: "To those who are under the law I became as one under the law, although I was not under it." Moreover, Christ in Matt. 17[:24-27], as he was about to pay the temple tax even though he was not obligated to do so, discussed with Peter whether taxes were paid by the children of kings or only by others. Peter answered, "Only by the others." Then Jesus said: "Thus, the children of kings are exempt from taxation. However, so that we give them no offense, go to the sea and cast out a line. Take the first fish you catch, and in his mouth you will find a penny. Give it for you and me."[39]

Here we see that works and other matters are free for a Christian through faith. And yet, because others still do not believe, individual Christians[q] take upon themselves and observe what they are not obligated to. Christians do it freely because they are certain that it surely pleases God. Moreover, they do it gladly, take it on themselves like any other free work that presents itself without their having chosen it. For they seek and desire nothing more than simply to act in faith in a way that pleases God.

38. For a similar argument, see *The Freedom of a Christian* below, p. 532.

39. Luther calls the coin a *pfennig*, a coin originally made of 1/240th of a pound of silver but often much less. In the sixteenth century, the coin could still be worth a substantial amount, depending on where it had been minted.

q   Singular in the original.

In this essay,[r] we have undertaken to teach which works are truly good and, in this section, which work is supreme. It is obvious that we are not talking about the second, third, or fourth kind of people, but about the first group, to which the others should aspire. The first group should, however, bear patiently with the others and instruct them. For this reason, one should not despise those still weak in faith, who would like to do good and learn better and still do not understand, on account of their ceremonies to which they cling so tightly. It is not as if they are completely lost. Instead, blame their ignorant and blind instructors, who never taught them faith and led them so deeply into works. Carefully and gradually, as if handling a sick person, they must once again be led out into faith but still be allowed for a while to cling to some works for the sake of their conscience and practice them as if necessary for salvation until they understand faith correctly. In this way, they will not be torn from these things so quickly lest their weak conscience be so completely destroyed or confused that they retain neither faith nor works. We should not, however, even bother with obstinate folk who are stuck in works and ignore what is said about faith and even fight against it. This Christ did and taught when he said [Matt. 15:14]: "Let them alone; they are blind guides of the blind."

16. You may ask, however: "How can I be sure that all my works are pleasing to God, since from time to time I fall short, for example, by talking, eating, drinking, or sleeping too much or by crossing the line in some other way, none of which I seem able to avoid?" The answer is: "Your question demonstrates that you consider faith to be like any work and fail to set it over all works. Faith is the highest and best work precisely because it persists and it erases everyday sins by not doubting that God is so well disposed toward you that such pitfalls and mistakes are, as it were, invisible,[s] even if a

r   In German, *sermo* was a loan word from Latin and could mean "sermon" or, as in this case, "essay."

s   Literally, "looks through his fingers," a favorite expression of Luther for God's toleration of human sin.

40. In the early church, murder, adultery, and apostasy were considered mortal sins, capable of killing the soul by making it liable to eternal damnation. By the Middle Ages, not only the so-called seven deadly sins (wrath, greed, sloth, pride, lust, envy, and gluttony) but any sin that a person deliberately committed was consider mortal sin.

mortal sin[40] were committed (although that should never, or at most seldom, happen to those whose lives are filled with faith and trust in God). Despite this, faith stands up again and does not doubt that its sin has already been removed, as it is written in 1 John 2[:1-2]: "I am writing this to you, my children, so that you may not sin. But if anyone does sin, then we have an advocate with God, Jesus Christ. He is the atonement for our sins." Moreover, Wisd. of Sol. 15[:2] states: "Even if we sin, we are still yours and acknowledge that you are great." And Prov. 24[:16]: "The righteous may fall seven times, but every time they rise again." For this reason, this trust and faith have to be so strong and exalted so that a person may know that before God's judgment seat all their works and their entire life are purely damnable sins, as it is written in Ps. 143[:2]: "No one living is righteous before you."[t] Moreover, such a person must be so uncertain about their works that they can only be good when they are done in this very faith, which does not expect judgment but only divine grace, favor, and mercy, as David says in Ps. 26[:3]: "For your mercy is forever before my eyes, and I walk cheerfully in your truth."[u] Again in Ps. 4[:6-7]: "The light of your countenance hovers over us," that is, the awareness of your grace through faith, and "with it you have made my heart glad," for we receive what we expect.

Now you see that works are blameless, forgiven, and good not by their own nature but by the mercy and grace of God for the sake of the faith that relies on this mercy. Because of works we can only be frightened, but because of God's grace we can comfort ourselves, as Ps. 147[:11] says: "The Lord takes pleasure in those who fear him and yet still trust in his mercy."[v] For this reason, we pray with complete trust, "our Father," and still ask "forgive us our debts"—his children and yet still sinners; we are precious to him and yet fail to

t   See thesis 3 of the *Heidelberg Disputation*, above, p. 89.

u   Luther and his contemporaries assumed that most if not all of the psalms were written by David.

v   In Luther's unique rendering of the psalm.

satisfy him.[41] Faith, fortified in the goodness and favor of God, does all of this.

17. You may ask, however, where faith and confidence come from or where they may be found. To know this is more necessary than anything else. First, without a doubt, it does not come from your works or merits but alone from Jesus Christ, who has freely promised it and bestows it, as St. Paul says in Rom. 5[:8]: "God makes his love so sweet and agreeable in that Christ died for us while we were still sinners." It is as if Paul wanted to say: "Does this not make for a strong and invincible confidence that Christ died for our sins even before we asked for it or were concerned about it, indeed, while we were still wandering further and further into sin?" Paul continues [5:9-10]: "If Christ died for us a long time ago, while we were still sinners, much more surely then will we be saved through him now that we have been justified by his blood. For if while we were still enemies we were reconciled with God through the death of his Son, we will certainly be saved by his life now that we are reconciled."

Look here! You must imprint Christ in yourself and see how God holds up his mercy before you, offering it without any prior merit on your part. From this picture of his grace you must derive faith and confidence that all your sins are forgiven. Thus, faith does not originate with works, nor do works manufacture faith. Instead, faith must spring and flow from the blood, wounds, and death of Christ.[42] When in this death you see that God is so loving to you that he even gave his Son for you,[w] then your heart simply melts[x] and in turn becomes pleasing to God. In this way confidence grows out of pure favor and love, that is, out of God's love for you and your love for God. We thus have never read that the Holy Spirit was given to anyone when he or she performed works but always when people heard the mercy of God and the gospel of Christ. Today and in every age, faith comes only from that same word and from nowhere else. For Christ

41. An expression of Luther's assertion that the believer is "simultaneously saint and sinner" (*simul iustus et peccator*).

This woodcut by Lucas Cranach the Elder is taken from the last printed leaf of the third Wittenberg printing of *Sermon on Good Works*. It shows the Apostle John, Mary the mother of Jesus, Mary Magdalene, and three soldiers gathered before the cross.

42. For this description of faith's origin, Luther borrows from the language of the so-called Christ-mysticism of the Middle Ages, found already in Bernard of Clairvaux (1090–1153) down to Johann von Staupitz (c. 1460–1524).

---

w   Cf. John 3:16.

x   Literally: becomes sweet.

43. Luther, like others, including the medieval commentator Paul of Burgos (c. 1351–1435), understood this passage as a prophecy of Christ. Later, following Nicholas of Lyra, Luther interpreted it as Moses' admonition to the Israelites (see LW 9:290–99).

44. This heading ("second good work") appears in the printed editions and encompasses four "good works" that fulfill the second commandment and are discussed in sections 21–31. Luther and later Lutherans numbered the Decalogue (Ten Commandments) according to the Greek Septuagint and Latin Vulgate, interpreting the command about graven images, which the Hebrew Bible and Reformed Christians count as the second commandment, as an expansion of the first commandment applicable only to the Israelites. See, e.g., *Against the Heavenly Prophets*, 1525 (LW 40:86).

is the rock from which a person sucks butter and honey, as Moses says in Deut. 32[:13].[43]

The Second Good Work [44]

18. Up to this point, we have treated the first work and the first commandment, but very briefly and in broad strokes since much more could be said. Now we move on to works related to the other commandments.

The second work, following immediately after faith, is prescribed by the second commandment that we should honor God's name and not use it in vain.[y] Like all other works, this one cannot be accomplished without faith, and if attempted without it, the result is pure hypocrisy and pretense. Next to faith, we can do nothing greater than to extol, preach, and sing God's praises, honor, and name, lifting them up and magnifying them in every way we can.

Although I said above (and it is true) that no differences exist among works in which faith is present and active, nevertheless this may be understood only when those works are measured against faith and its work. If, however, works are compared with one another, then differences do exist and one is greater than another. Just as in the body, when its members are considered together and measured against the health of the entire body, there is no difference among them and all are equally healthy; but still there is a difference among the works of individual members, and one work is greater, nobler, and more useful than another. In this case as well, to praise God's honor and name is a greater work than those that fulfill the commandments that follow. Nonetheless, both this work and those that follow must proceed from the very same faith.

I know full well that this work has been so devalued as to have become almost unknown. We will therefore examine it further. Moreover, it cannot be stressed enough that this work must be done in the faith and confidence that it pleases

y　Exod. 20:7; Deut. 5:11.

God very much. In fact, there is no other work in which trust and faith are experienced and felt so noticeably as in giving honor to God's name. It also helps strengthen and increase faith, although all the other works help as well, as St. Peter says in 2 Pet. 1[:10]: "Dear brothers [and sisters], be diligent to confirm your call and election through good works."[z]

19. The first commandment forbids us to have other gods. As a consequence, it commands us to have the one true God by means of firm faith, trust, confidence, hope, and love.[45] With these works alone can we possess, honor, and hold fast to the one God. No other work enables us to draw close to God or depart from God. This only happens through faith or unbelief, through trust or doubt. No other work ever reaches up to God. In the same way, the second commandment prohibits us from taking God's name in vain. But that is not all. It also commands us to honor, invoke, praise, proclaim, and exalt his name. That is to say, it is not possible to avoid dishonoring God's name when it is not properly honored. For although it may be honored with the mouth, genuflections, kisses,[a] or other actions, when they do not proceed from the heart through faith, trusting God's favor, the result is nothing but pretense and a hypocritical appearance.

See how many good works a person can do all day long in this commandment and never be without the good works of this commandment, even if undertaking no more pilgrimages or visits to shrines.[46] So tell me, does a moment ever pass in which we do not continuously receive God's blessings or suffer evil misfortune? What are these things but constant admonitions and encouragements to praise, honor, and bless God and to call upon him and his name? Even if you did nothing in other matters, would you not have enough to do with this commandment alone by blessing, singing to, praising, and honoring God's name unceasingly?

45. Here, as elsewhere, Luther insists that a negative (or, elsewhere, positive) command always implies the opposite. See his explanations of the Decalogue in the *Large Catechism* and *Small Catechism*.

46. A person could visit countless local shrines, many of which honored the Virgin Mary or a local saint. There were also more famous pilgrimage sites, such as St. James in Santiago de Compostela and the tombs of the apostles in Rome.

---

z   The phrase "through good works" is from the Latin Vulgate. It did not appear in Erasmus's version of the Greek text (an absence mentioned in Erasmus's annotations) and, thus, not in Luther's 1522 German translation of the New Testament.

a   By kissing crosses, relics, or images.

Why else were tongue, voice, language, and mouth created? As Ps. 51[:14-15] says: "Lord, open my lips and my mouth will declare your praise," and "My tongue shall lift up your mercy." Is there any work done in heaven besides the second commandment, as we read in Ps. 84[:4]: "Happy are those who live in your house and forever sing your praise."[b] David indicates the same in Ps. 34[:1]: "God's praise shall continually be in my mouth." And St. Paul says in 1 Cor. 10[:31]: "Whether you eat or drink or whatever you do, do it all to the honor of God." Likewise Col. 3[:17]: "Whatever you do, in word or deed, do it in the name of the Lord Jesus Christ, giving thanks and praise to God the Father." If we took the work of this commandment to heart, we would have heaven on earth and enough to do forever, just like the blessed in heaven.

20. From this arises the astonishing but just judgment of God, that sometimes a poor person, whom no one can imagine doing many and great works, when at home alone praises God joyfully when things are going well or calls upon God with complete confidence when something bad happens. In so doing that individual performs a greater, more God-pleasing work than another person who frequently fasts, prays, endows churches, makes pilgrimages, and is busy doing great deeds everywhere. Such a fool gawks and looks for even greater works to the point of being so completely blinded as to miss the greatest work of all. In the eyes of such fools,[c] praising God is a very small thing in contrast to the fabulous image of these self-invented works, in which such individuals presumably praise themselves more than God or which please them more than God does. With their good works they rage against the second commandment and its works. The Pharisees and the public sinner in the Gospel [Luke 18:9-14] offer examples of both. In his transgressions, the sinner invokes and praises God, thus fulfilling the two greatest commandments, to believe in and honor God. The hypocrite fails to do either and parades

---

b   Luther interprets this psalm anagogically as a description of heaven.

c   Singular in the original.

around with other works through which he extols himself more than God and puts more trust in himself than in God. Rightly, therefore, the hypocrite is deservedly rejected while the sinner is chosen.

This happens all the time, that the greater and better the works, the less pretentious they are, so that everyone thinks they are easy to do because it appears that almost no one gives more of an impression of extolling God's name and honor like those who in reality are not doing it. With such hypocrisy—since their hearts lack faith—they make the most precious work despicable. In Rom. 2[:23-24] the Apostle Paul dares to say openly that those who blaspheme God's name the most [are] those who boast of the law of God. It is easy to speak God's name and to record his glory on paper and walls; but to praise God completely, to bless him for his benevolence, to call upon him for consolation in every distress—these are, next to faith, truly the greatest and rarest of works. When we realize how seldom they are encountered in Christendom, our sadness might make us despair. Despite this, the grand, beautiful, and glorious works devised by human imagination keep multiplying; superficially they appear identical to genuine works, but below the surface they lack faith and trust and, in short, have nothing good about them. For this reason, Isa. 48[:1] also admonishes the people: "Listen up, you who bear the name as if you truly were Israel, you who swear by the name of God but do not pay homage to him with truth and righteousness." That is, they did not do it with genuine faith and trust (which are the real "truth and righteousness") but were trusting in themselves, their works, and their own abilities, all the while invoking and praising the name of God. These two things,[47] however, cannot be reconciled with each other.

21. The first work of this commandment is thus to praise God for all his benefits, which are so numerous that such praise and thanksgiving would have neither interruptions nor an end. For who could praise God adequately for our physical existence, to say nothing of all the temporal and eternal blessings? As a result, through one part of this commandment, everybody is inundated with good and precious

47. Trusting oneself and yet invoking God's name.

works. If they[d] do them with genuine faith, they have in no way existed [on earth] in vain. By contrast, no one sins more gravely than the worst hypocritical holy folk, who please themselves and who like to boast and to hear the world praise, honor, and extol them.

It follows, then, that the second work of this commandment is to guard yourself against all worldly honor and praise, avoiding and fleeing from them, seeking nothing for your own name, reputation, and acclaim so that everyone would talk about you and sing your praises. This is a dangerous sin but still one of the most common despite its being regarded as a minor offense. Everyone, no matter how insignificant, wants to count for something and not be the least of all, so deep is the corruption of human nature in its conceit and false trust in itself, contrary to the first and the second commandments.

Because in this world people consider this horrible offense to be the noblest virtue, it is perilous for them to read pagan books or listen to pagan stories if they are not already well acquainted with God's commandments and stories from Holy Scripture. All pagan books are suffused with this poison of seeking praise and honor. A person learns from them in accord with blind reason: people cannot be or become capable and reputable unless motivated by praise and honor. Nor can they be ranked among the best if they do not chase after glory and honor above everything else: body, life, friends, and possessions. All the holy fathers[48] have denounced this vice and unanimously decided that it is the most difficult of all to overcome. According to St. Augustine, all other vices are expressed in evil deeds, but pride and vanity express themselves in good works.[e]

If therefore people[f] had nothing else to do except this second work of this commandment, they would have more than enough to do for a lifetime, in battling this vice that is

48. Early church theologians, including the four doctors of the Western church: Ambrose (c. 340–397), St. Augustine, St. Jerome (c. 347–420), and Pope Gregory I (c. 540–604).

---

d   Singular in the original.

e   A paraphrase of a statement attributed to Augustine by Prosper of Aquitaine (c. 390–c. 455), *Sententiae ex operibus S. Augustini* (MPL 45, col. 1863).

f   Singular in the original.

so widespread, sneaky, and slippery, and so hard to uproot. We, however, turn our backs on this good work and practice other lesser good works and by so doing even toss this one aside and forget it completely. In this way, the holy name of God, which alone ought to be honored, is dishonored and taken in vain by our own accursed name, self-satisfaction, and desire for fame. In God's eyes, this sin is graver than murder and adultery, but the evil it harbors is harder to discern than murder because of its subtlety since this happens in the spirit, not in the crude flesh.

22. According to some people, it is well for young people to do good deeds when they are motivated by fame and honor or, on the contrary, by shame and disgrace. For there are many who do good and avoid evil out of love of honor and fear of shame and in no way would have behaved otherwise. I will let them think what they want. Now, however, we are looking for how a person ought to do truly good works. Thus, those who are so disposed need not be motivated by fear of shame or by love of honor. Instead, they have and should have a better and much nobler impetus, namely, the commandment of God, the fear of God, the favor of God, along with their faith in and love of God. Those who lack this impetus or despise it and let themselves be driven by shame or honor receive their reward, as the Lord says in Matt. 6[:2, 5]. In their case, the deed and the reward correspond to the motivation, and there is nothing good about it except in the eyes of the world.

In my opinion, however, one can habituate and drive a young person [to good behavior] more easily with the fear of God and the divine commandments than anything else. When that does not work, we have to put up with other motivations like shame and honor to get a young person to do good and avoid evil. In the same way, we must tolerate the sinful or imperfect people described above.[g] We can do no more than to tell them: "What you are doing is neither right nor sufficient in the eyes of God" and let them go until they also learn to do good for the sake of God's commandment.

g   See above, p. 281f.

This is just how small children, by means of rewards and promises from their parents, are encouraged to pray, fast, learn, and so on. It would not be desirable, however, for children to be impelled like that all their lives and never to learn to do good in the fear of God or, worse yet, to become so accustomed to doing it only for the sake of praise and honor.

23. It is true, however, that we must still have a good name and reputation, and everyone should behave so that no one speaks ill of them or is offended by them, as St. Paul says in Rom. 12[:17]: "We should be diligent to do good not only before God but in the sight of all."[h] And in 2 Cor. 4[:2]: "We have such integrity that no one can find anything wrong with us." Great diligence and caution must prevail here, however, so that honor and a good name do not lead to a swollen head that is overly pleased with itself.[49] The saying of Solomon [Prov. 27:21] applies here: "As the fire in the furnace tests gold, so a person is tested by being praised." There are only a few, highly spiritual people who, in the presence of honor and praise, remain free and serene and unaffected. They are not bothered by it and develop no conceit; instead, they remain unencumbered, attributing all of their honor and good name to God alone, letting God be responsible for them and using them only to honor God and to improve the lives of others instead of using them for their own advantage. As a result, they do not measure themselves against or place themselves above the least capable and most despised people on earth, but they regard themselves as God's servants to whom God has granted the honor of serving both God and their neighbors. This is no different than if God had commanded them, for God's sake, to distribute a few precious coins among the poor. Jesus says therefore in Matt. 5[:16]: "Let your light shine before others so that they may see your good works and give glory to your Father in heaven." He does not say "they should give glory and praise to you" but rather, "your work should only serve to improve their lives so that they will praise God both in themselves and in you." This is the proper use of a good name and respect: when God

49. Luther reflects here many aspects of Augustinian and monastic humility.

---

h   Luther conflates 2 Cor. 8:20-21 with Rom. 12:17.

is praised through the betterment of others. If people want to praise us, however, instead of God in us, we should not tolerate it and with all our might guard ourselves against this sin, fleeing from it at all costs as from the severest sin and thievery of divine honor.

24. This is why God many times allows individuals[i] to fall into grave sin, and even to remain there, so that they may become dishonored in their own eyes and others'. Otherwise, had they survived with their great gifts and virtues intact, they might not have avoided the formidable vice of [trusting] their pure honor and reputation. God, so to speak, protects us from this sin using other serious sins, so that his holy name alone remains honored. Thus, because of our twisted depravity, which not only does what is evil but also misuses all that is good, one sin becomes the medicine to heal another.[50]

See how much individuals[j] have to do if they want to perform good works, for countless opportunities surround them all the time! And see how they squander [these opportunities] everywhere and blindly ignore them, and seek and pursue other works according to their own thoughts and pleasure, so that no one can speak against this enough nor find enough protection against it. All the prophets had to deal with this, and some were even killed simply because they condemned these very self-made works[51] and only proclaimed God's command. One of them, Jeremiah, says in chapter 7[:21-23]: "Take your burnt offerings and add them to your sacrifices and eat their flesh. I have not commanded anything like that, but I have commanded you to listen to my voice"—that is, do not listen to what you imagine is correct and good but to what I command you—"and walk only in the way that I have commanded you." And in Deut. 12[:8, 32]: "You shall not do what appears right and good to you, but that which your God has commanded."

These verses and countless others are intended to tear people away not only from their sins but also from the works

50. Because Luther is arguing that, next to faith, honoring God's reputation is the highest Christian work, he can say that other sins that cause shame cure the (worse) sin of conceit.

51. Cf. Col. 2:23 ("self-chosen spirituality"), which Luther contrasts to works commanded by God.

---

i   Singular in the original.
j   Singular in the original.

that they imagine are good and to direct them instead to the simple meaning of God's commandments, so that at all times they diligently heed them alone. As it is written in Exod. 13[:9]: "You shall let these commandments be a sign on your hand and a constant image before your eyes." And, Ps. 1[:2]: "Upright persons speak to themselves, day and night about God's commandment."[k] We have more than enough to do, indeed too much, if we are simply to satisfy the divine commandments. God has given them to us, so that when we comprehend them we will not be idle for a second and can rightly forget all other works. But the evil spirit, who never rests, when unable to lead us into committing evil works on the left side, attacks us on the right with our own self-fabricated works that appear good. Against both, God has commanded in Deut. 28[:14] and Josh. 23[:6], "You shall not depart from my commandments either to the right or to the left."

25. The third work of this commandment is to call on God's name in all distress. For this greatly reveres God's name and keeps it holy: that we invoke it and call upon it when under affliction or in distress.[l] This, finally, is the reason God inflicts us with suffering, affliction, distress, and even death and lets us live with many sinful urges so that through them he may impel us and cause us to run to him, cry out, and call upon his holy name. By so doing, we perform this work of the second commandment, as God says in Ps. 50[:14, 15]: "Call upon me in your distress and I will help you," and "You shall venerate me for I desire a sacrifice of praise."[m] For this reason, this is the way through which we may come to salvation, for through this work a person discovers and experiences what God's name is and how power-

---

k   In the singular in the original. Luther paraphrases the word *meditate* according to the Hebrew "speak to oneself."

l   German: *anfechtung und nodt,* two crucial terms for Luther's lifelong view of the Christian life as under assault and beset by direst needs, and thus obliged to pray. He often links the second commandment, prayer, and especially the first petition of the Lord's Prayer.

m   Luther also cites this in the LC, "Lord's Prayer," par. 19 (BC, 434).

ful it is in helping everyone who calls upon it. Through this, our trust and faith will grow very strong and thereby will also fulfill the first and greatest commandment. David experienced this, in Ps. 54[:6-7]: "You have delivered me from all distress; therefore I will make known your name and declare that it is lovely and sweet." And in Ps. 91[:14-15] God says: "I will deliver them because they hope in me; I will aid them because they have acknowledged my name."

Look here! Is there a person on earth who would not have enough to do regarding this work to last a lifetime? Who is not under attack every hour? I will skip over those countless attacks caused by adversities. The most pernicious kind comes when there is no attack at all and everything is running smoothly, lest in such a situation the person forgets God and through lack of restraint misuses the good times. Here it is ten times more necessary to call upon God's name than in the midst of adversity. As it is written in Ps. 91[:7]: "A thousand may fall at your left hand, ten thousand at your right hand." Everyday human experience shows us as plain as day that horrible sins and vices flourish more during good times when there is peace and things are cheap than when we are afflicted by war, pestilence, sickness, and other misfortune. For example, Moses feared for his people, that there would be no greater cause for them to forsake God's commandments than that they became too stuffed and had too much leisure, as he says in Deut. 32[:15]: "My dear people have become rich, sated, and fat; therefore they have turned against their God." Consequently, God also allowed many of their enemies to survive and refused to drive them away, so that the people could not relax but had to keep practicing the commandments, as is described in Judg. 3[:1-5]. God is dealing with us in the same manner when he allows us to suffer all kinds of misfortune. He is so concerned about us that he teaches us, indeed drives us, to honor and call upon his name, to gain faith and trust in him and thereby to fulfill the first two commandments.

26. Here foolish people behave dangerously, especially self-righteous, holier-than-thou folk and all those who desire to be something special. They promote the use of

52. Pious phrases, alleged to have come from heaven and sometimes worn as amulets for protection against personal harm, illness, or death.

53. Practices quite common in Luther's day and universally condemned by Christian teachers.

incantations; some people shield themselves with [heavenly] letters,[52] others seek out fortune-tellers, some search for one thing, others for another, all in order to be safe and avoid misfortune. Words alone cannot describe the devilish specter that reigns in this game, through magic, conjuring, and superstition,[53] all of which occurs because people simply have no need of God's name and trust God in nothing. Here God's name and the first two commandments are greatly dishonored, because they seek from the devil, other people, and creatures what they ought to seek and find in God alone through a pure, simple faith, trust, joyous hope, and invocation of God's holy name.

Now judge for yourself whether or not it is a fatuous perversion that some people have to believe in the devil, other people, or some creature and trust them for good fortune and have nothing to fall back on for help except this kind of faith and trust. What remuneration should God, who is true and just, offer people so that they trust God as much as or more than other people and the devil? He not only promises help and solid support but also commands us to count on it, and he gives us all kinds of reasons and prods us to put our faith and trust in him. Is this not a terrible pity both that either the devil or human beings, who command and force nothing but only make promises and give assurances, are set over God, who actually promises, urges, and commands, and that they are held in greater esteem than God? We should rightly be ashamed and learn a lesson from those who have faith in the devil or human beings. For if the devil, who is an evil, deceitful spirit, keeps faith with those who ally themselves with him, how much more, incomparably more, will the most benevolent and faithful God stay true to anyone who trusts him? A rich man trusts and relies upon his money and property, and are we unwilling to trust and rely on the living God and believe that he can and will help us? As they say, "Gold makes bold,"*n* as Bar. 3[:17] states: "Gold is something in which people put their trust." Much

---

n   A German proverb: "*Gut macht Mut!*" literally, "Possessions make [a person have] courage."

greater, however, is the boldness created by the eternal and highest Good, on which none but the children of God rely.

27. Even if none of these adversities° compelled us to trust and call upon God, sin alone would be more than sufficient to make us practice this work. Sin besieges us with three mighty armies—our own flesh, the world, and the evil spirit—which harry and attack us without respite. God uses them to cause us constantly to do good works, that is, to do battle against sin and these enemies. The flesh seeks titillation and leisure; the world seeks wealth, favor, power, and acclaim; the evil spirit looks for arrogance, fame, conceit, and disdain of others.

Together they are so potent that even one of them is enough to overpower a person. And yet we can without a doubt overcome them but only by calling upon the holy name of God with a firm faith, as Solomon says in Prov. 18[:10]: "The name of God is a strong tower; the faithful flee to it and are lifted up." Thus, David says in Ps. 116[:13]: "I will drink the cup of salvation and call upon God's name." Again in Ps. 18[:3]: "I will call upon God with praise, so shall I be saved from all my enemies." We have become ignorant of these works and the strength of the divine name, because we are unaccustomed ever to struggle earnestly with sin and therefore to have need of God's name. This causes us to practice only our self-contrived works, which we are able to perform through our own powers.

28. Also included among the works of this commandment are the following: that we should not swear, curse, lie, deceive, or practice magic using God's holy name, or misuse it in any other way. These are crude examples with which everyone is familiar, but until now these sins were for the most part the only ones named in preaching and proclamation. Included here is also preventing others from lying, swearing, deceiving, cursing, practicing magic, or committing other sins using God's name. These are all good reasons to do good and to guard against evil.

---

o See par. 25 above.

54. Here Luther reflects his own behavior toward his opponents. In the *Large Catechism* Luther ties this criticism to both the second and eighth commandments. See *Large Catechism*, "Ten Commandments," pars. 54, 284 (BC, 393, 424).

55. The *summum bonum*, the most desirable purpose and goal of human existence, a concept derived from Greek philosophy that Christian theologians applied in various ways to life in God or eternal blessedness.

The most important and difficult work of this commandment[54] is to protect God's holy name against all those who misuse it spiritually and spread such misuse everywhere. It is not enough for me to praise the divine name for myself alone or to call upon it in good and bad times just for me. I must step forward and for the sake of God's name and honor take upon myself the hostility of everyone else, as Christ said to his disciples [Matt. 10:22]: "You will be hated by all because of my name." We cannot help but bring upon ourselves the anger of father, mother, and our best friends. In this matter, we must confront the authorities, both spiritual and temporal, and be rebuked as disobedient. Indeed, everyone the world admires—the rich, the learned, the holy—will turn against us. And although particularly those who are charged with preaching God's word are under this obligation, it is also expected of every Christian when circumstances demand it. In fact, we should invest all that we have on behalf of God's holy name and prove with our actions both that we love God and his name, his honor and his glory, above anything else and that we trust God above all things and expect all our blessings from him. In this way, we confess publicly that we consider God as the highest good[55] and for his sake forsake and leave behind all other goods.

29. First of all, we must strive against all injustice when the truth or righteousness is impugned by force and adversity. We must not make any distinction here among persons, as some do who fight with great diligence and persistence against injustice that has been done to the rich and powerful or to their friends but remain silent and passive when it happens to the poor and despised or to their enemies. They do not see the name and honor of God as they really are but look through rose-colored glasses[p] and measure truth and justice according to the people affected. They will never be aware of their distorted vision because they privilege the person over the matter itself. They are arch-hypocrites and only appear to defend the truth. They realize they run no risk when they support the rich, the powerful, the learned,

p Literally, painted glass.

or their friends, who in turn will protect, respect, and otherwise be useful to them. It is very easy, therefore, to protest injustices done to popes, kings, princes, bishops, and other bigwigs. In these situations that are not so dire, everyone wants to show how righteous they are. Alas, how insidious is the false Adam with his petitions![56] How finely he dresses up his desire for self-advancement in the garb of truth, justice, and divine honor! When, however, something bad happens to a poor and insignificant person, this false pair of eyes sees no advantage to be gained but only a threat of losing favor with the powerful. Thus, such a one prudently leaves the poor person without aid. Who can describe how much this depravity has corrupted Christendom? God declares in Ps. 82[:2-4]: "How long will you judge unjustly and show partiality to the wicked? Give justice to the poor and the orphan; give the afflicted and the destitute their due. Rescue the needy and forsaken; deliver them from the hand of the wicked." But no one does this, and thus the psalm continues [v. 5]: "They have neither knowledge nor understanding and walk around in darkness." That is, they do not see the truth but cling only to the reputation with the bigwigs regardless of how unjust they are and ignore the poor even if justice is all on their side.

30. See how many good works are close at hand here! The vast majority of the rich, the powerful and "friends," act unjustly and oppress the poor, the forgotten, and their opponents. The more powerful they are, the more despicable their actions. If they cannot be resisted with force in order to assist the truth, then we should at least speak the truth publicly and bolster it with words, not giving our consent to what they do or implying that it is just but instead stating the truth openly.

What benefit would individuals[q] gain from doing all kinds of good things, like visiting Rome and other holy places, acquiring every indulgence, or endowing all church buildings and other religious foundations,[57r] if they were

56. That is, the old creature: Human nature in bondage to sin.

57. Luther's own prince, Elector Frederick, had seen to extensive renovations of the All Saints' Foundation and Church in Wittenberg. Money or income from land holdings were to fund such foundations, the members of which might be responsible to recite private Masses for the dead, teach at universities, or the like.

q   Singular in the original.
r   German: *alle kirchenn unnd stiffte.*

found guilty, in the name and honor of God, of silencing and forsaking that very name and instead considering their possessions, reputation, connections, and friends more important than the truth, which is God's very name and honor? To whom does this good work not come knocking at the door daily, with the result that it is unnecessary to roam far from home or inquire where good works can be found? When we consider how people everywhere live so rashly and frivolously in regard to this matter, then with the prophet we have to exclaim: *Omnis homo mendax!* "Every human being is false, lies, and deceives."[5] For they set aside the true, central good works and adorn and paint themselves with the least important, using them to look righteous and quietly to pave their way into heaven.

You may ask: why does God not do this himself since God obviously knows how to and can help every person? God certainly can do this but prefers not to do it alone. God wants us to work together with him and does us the honor of desiring to accomplish his work with and through us. If we decline to accept this honor, then God will do it alone and help the poor. Those people, however, who did not wish to help God and scorned that great honor God will condemn along with all the unrighteous and consider as supporters of the unrighteous. Although God alone is blessed, he still wants to give us the honor and not be blessed by himself but share that blessedness with him. Were God to act alone, then the commandments would be given to us in vain, because no one would have cause to exercise themselves in the great works of these very commandments. Nor would anyone make an effort to view God and his name as the greatest good or to stake everything on him.

31. It also belongs to this work to oppose all false, seductive, errant, and heretical teachings and any abuse of the clerical authority. This is extremely serious because these teachings use God's holy name to fight against God's name. Thus, to oppose these people looks daunting and

---

5   "Every person is a liar." From the Vulgate reading of Ps. 116:11, which Luther renders freely in German. See also Rom. 3:4.

risky, because they claim that whoever opposes them also opposes God and all the saints, in whose seat these people claim to sit[58] and wield authority. They allege that the words of Christ were spoken to them: "Whoever hears you hears me; whoever rejects you rejects me."[59][t] They rely strictly on these words and have no compunction about saying, doing, or not doing whatever they want. They ban, curse, rob, kill, and perpetrate all the evildoings as they please without any restraint.[60] In no way did Christ mean that we should obey them in everything they say and do but only when they speak his word, the gospel, and not their own words and do his work and not their own. Otherwise how could we know whether or not to avoid their lies and sins? There must certainly be a rule that tells us to what extent we should obey and follow them—a rule that cannot be set by them but must be set over them by God according to which we can judge, as we shall hear in the fourth commandment."

Thus, at present, it must needs be the case that most of the clergy[v] preach false doctrine and abuse their spiritual authority, so that we have reason to do the work of this commandment. And we are being put to the test concerning what we will do or leave undone against such blasphemers for the sake of God's honor.

If only we were conscientious [about doing this], how often the official buffoons would impose their papal and episcopal excommunications in vain and how those Roman thunderbolts would be reduced to a whisper![61] How often would some people, to whom the world now has to listen, be forced to shut their mouths. How few preachers would be found in Christendom! But things have gotten to the point that whatever they claim must all be right. Now no one fights for God's name and honor, and I hold that there is no graver or more widespread sin in the public matters than this one.[62] For it is so difficult that, given the risk,

58. This paragraph reflects Luther's case with Rome. The papacy laid claim to be the successor to Peter and his see in Rome. See also 2 Thess. 2:4, which Luther took as a reference to anti-Christ.

59. This text played an important role in discussions of clerical authority throughout the Reformation. See, e.g., the *Augsburg Confession* XXVIII.21–28 (BC, 94–95).

60. Luther here is reflecting both common complaints about abuse of clerical power and his own particular struggle with the Roman hierarchy.

61. That is, papal decrees would have little effect. In October 1520, Luther would receive the official papal bull threatening excommunication, *Exsurge Domini*.

62. Namely, the sin of not opposing such misuse of God's name. Luther here is setting up a defense of his own outspoken criticisms of the papacy and its defenders.

---

t Luke 10:16.

u See below, pp. 337–41.

v Here and elsewhere, literally, "the spiritual estate," the common designation of the entire clergy.

few understand how to attack when armed only with God's name and power. But the prophets in ages past and the apostles (St. Paul especially) were masters at it. It did not bother them whether the most or least important priest said or did something in God's name or his own. They focused on the words and actions and held them up against God's commandment regardless of who spoke or acted—a big fish or a small fry[w]—in the name of God or some human being. For that reason, the apostles and prophets had to die, and in our day there would be much more to say [against such people] because it is much worse now. But Christ and Saints Peter and Paul are forced to adorn all of this [teaching] with their holy names, with the result that no more ignominious name exists on earth than the holiest and exalted name of Jesus Christ.[63]

By itself, this abuse and blasphemy against God's holy name ought to scare people to death, and I fear that if it keeps up, we will start openly worshiping the devil as a god, given that the clerical authorities and scholars continue to handle these matters with such indescribable coarseness. It is high time that we earnestly ask God to make his name holy. But blood will be the price, and those who now sit among the holy martyrs' possessions, having gained it through the martyrs' blood, must themselves now make martyrs. More about that at another time.[64]

On the Third Commandment[65]

1. We have just seen how many good works are contained in the second commandment, but they are not good in and of themselves but only when they are done in faith and with confidence in divine benevolence.[x] And we see now how much we have to do when we observe only this commandment and how many others, who do not understand this

63. Luther is arguing that present false teaching uses Christ's and the apostles' names for legitimacy. The popes claimed to be successors to Peter and Paul, whose basilica in Rome was the object of the money raised by the Peter Indulgence.

64. Luther is intimating that the papacy has become demonic to the point of making new martyrs while living off the reputation of the church's early martyrs. See his *Address to the Christian Nobility* (p. 435f) and *The Babylonian Captivity of the Church* (LW 36:11–18), both written later in 1520.

65. The heading for this section specifies the commandment instead of the work or works of the commandment as in previous headings. The numbering of the subsections starts over as Luther moves through the commandments in order. See Exod. 20:8 and Deut. 5:12: "Remember the sabbath day and keep it holy."

w   Literally, "a big Hans or a small Nick."
x   A reference back to the first commandment.

commandment, unfortunately busy themselves with other works. Now comes the third commandment: "You shall keep the Sabbath holy." How our hearts should behave toward God in thoughts is commanded in the first commandment, and how the mouth should behave in words is commanded in the second. In the third commandment is commanded how we should behave toward God in our deeds. These commandments are written on the first tablet of the law of Moses that he held in his right hand and that govern human beings on the right side, that is, in those matters relating to God which concern God's dealings with humans and humans' with God apart from the mediation of any creature.[66]

The first work of this commandment, which we commonly called worship,[y] is unsophisticated and easily grasped: attending Mass, praying, and listening to the sermon on Sundays and holy days.[67] According to this definition, this commandment entails only a few works. If, however, they are not done with faith and trust in God's goodwill, they are nothing, as we said earlier. Consequently, it would really be good if there were fewer holy days, especially since in our day those activities—killing time, eating and drinking too much, playing games, and doing other evil deeds—are for the most part worse than what we do on workdays.[68] In addition, attending Mass and hearing a sermon have no positive effect on people, and the prayers are said without faith. It has almost come to the point where people think it is enough that we watch the Mass with our eyes, hear the sermon with our ears, and say the prayers with our lips. It is all external, so that we do not consider that we receive something from the Mass into our hearts; learn and retain something from the sermon; and seek, desire, and expect something from prayer. True, the bishops, priests, and those responsible for preaching[69] are even more at fault because they fail to preach the gospel or teach people how they ought to view the Mass, listen to the sermon, and say their prayers. For that reason, we will treat each of these works in more detail.

66. The Bible mentions two tablets but not a division into three and seven commandments that were inscribed on the tablets. The division apparently originated in rabbinic Judaism.

67. In later expositions of the Ten Commandments, Luther associates prayer exclusively with the second commandment. Here he highlights corporate prayer. Throughout this tract, Luther uses the word *Mass* to denote the regular Sunday worship with preaching, readings, prayers, and the Lord's Supper.

68. Before the Reformation, the major and minor festivals of the church year had become so numerous that attempts were made in certain regions to prune the calendar. See LW 53:14 (WA 12:37).

69. In Luther's day, bishop, priest, and preacher were three chief clerical offices in the church.

y   The German word is *Gottesdienst*, literally, "the service of God." The second "work" of this commandment begins below, p. 321.

70. Luther will take up some of these themes later in the year in the *Babylonian Captivity of the Church* (LW 36:3–126, esp. 37–44).

71. Luther uses the term for an endowed Mass that was said yearly on the date of someone's death but to refer to Christ's institution at the last supper and therefore all celebrations of the Lord's Supper.

72. "Under" means "under the forms of bread and wine," based upon a Latin formulation used by the Fourth Lateran Council (1215) to denote that the body and blood of Christ were contained under the forms (*species*) of bread and wine. For Luther's explanation of the Supper as a testament and for his rejection of this philosophical explanation for Christ's presence in the Supper, called transubstantiation, see *The Babylonian Captivity* (LW 36:28–35).

2. At Mass, it is necessary that we be present with our heart as well; this happens when we practice faith in our hearts. We have to repeat the words that Christ spoke when he instituted the Mass: "'Take and eat; this is my body given for you.' In the same manner, he took the cup and said: 'Take and drink from it, all of you; that is a new, eternal covenant in my blood, which is poured out for you and for many for the forgiveness of sins. As often as you drink it, do it in remembrance of me.'"[70,z] With these words, Christ established for himself a memorial or anniversary Mass[71] to be celebrated for him daily throughout Christendom. And he attached to it a glorious, rich, and generous will and testament, which grants and establishes for us not annuities, money, or worldly possessions but the forgiveness of all our sins, grace, and mercy unto eternal life, so that everyone who comes to this memorial shall possess this testament. Christ has died so that the testament became durable and irrevocable. Instead of leaving us a sealed document, he has left us as a proper sign and "legal instrument" his own body and blood under the bread and wine.[72]

It is necessary for individuals[a] to practice the first work of this commandment properly in that they not doubt that it is a testament and a trustworthy one at that, so that they do not make Christ into a liar. If you do nothing at Mass but stand there without realizing or believing that through this testament Christ has promised and bestowed the forgiveness of all your sins, how is that different from saying: "I do not know or I do not believe that forgiveness of my sins is promised and bestowed here"? Countless Masses are now said throughout the world, but very few hear them with this kind of faith and practice! It provokes God's anger, and as a result, none can participate in the Mass fruitfully except for those[b] who are disconsolate, yearn for divine grace, and desire to be rid of their sins or even for those with an evil

---

z   A conflation of Matt. 26:26-28 and 1 Cor. 11:23-25, reflecting the text of the Latin Mass in Luther's day.

a   Singular in the original.

b   Singular in the original.

intention [to sin],[73] as long as they are transformed during the Mass and desire the benefits of this testament. For that reason, in former times [only] notorious, public sinners were not admitted to the Mass.[74]

When, however, this faith is in order, the heart draws joy from the testament, warms itself in God's love to the point of melting. Then, praise and thanksgiving follow with a sweetened heart.[75] For this reason, the Greek word for "mass" is *Eucharist*, or "thanksgiving." We should praise and thank God for such a consoling, rich, and sublime testament, just as a person would exult, be thankful, and rejoice for inheriting a thousand gulden or more from a friend.[c] All too often, however, Christ receives the same response as those who have made people rich through their wills. The heirs quickly forget them, and they never receive praise or thanks for what they did. The same happens now with our Masses: they are merely celebrated, but we do not know why or what purpose they serve. We do not thank, love, or praise but remain barren and hardened, and just continue saying our little prayers.[76] More about this at another time.[d]

3. The sermon should be nothing other than the proclamation of this testament. But who will hear it if no one proclaims it, and those who should be preaching it scarcely comprehend it themselves! The sermons wander around in completely useless fables with the result that Christ is forgotten. Our situation is similar to that of the man in 2 Kgs. 7[:19]: "We see our goods, but we cannot enjoy them." Eccles. [6:1-2] also refers to it: "It is a great misfortune when God gives people riches but does not allow them to be enjoyed." We see innumerable Masses but do not know whether they are testaments or something else entirely, as if they were run-of-the-mill good works in and of themselves. O God, how totally blinded we are! Wherever this testament is rightly preached, however, it is necessary that we listen attentively, comprehend and retain it, continually meditate on it, and

73. As in the *Explanations of the Ninety-Five Theses* (LW 31:106–7), Luther insists that the sacraments are precisely intended for true sinners. For this he was condemned in the papal bull of excommunication. See Luther's response in LW 32:12-19.

74. They were not allowed to receive Communion, and in early Christianity they were not permitted to attend Mass or were restricted to an area away from the assembly of worshipers.

75. Here and elsewhere Luther uses highly emotive language, often found in late medieval German mystical writings as well as in later Lutheran hymnody.

76. Luther is referring to the common late medieval practice of practicing private devotions during the Mass. The Mass bells would then ring to get people to focus on the Mass at the crucial moments of transubstantiation and elevation (when the unbloodied sacrifice of Christ was offered to the Father).

c   That is, millions of dollars.
d   Namely, in *The Babylonian Captivity of the Church* (LW 36:3–126), which was published later in 1520.

thereby strengthen faith against all attacks of sin—past, present, or future.

This is the only ceremony or practice that Christ instituted in which Christians are to assemble, practice, and hold in harmony. Unlike other ceremonies, Christ has not permitted this one to be a mere work but instead placed in it an abundant and overflowing treasure, which is offered to and possessed by all who believe in it.

The sermon should entice sinners to feel remorse for their sin and inflame the desire for this treasure. It follows that it must be a grave sin for those who do not listen to the gospel and spurn this treasure and the rich meal to which they are invited. A much graver sin, however, is committed by those who do not preach the gospel and thereby allow those who would gladly have heard it go to ruin, although Christ has steadfastly commanded them to preach the gospel and this testament. In fact, he did not want the Mass to be celebrated unless the gospel was also preached. Thus he says: "As often as you do it, do it in remembrance of me." That is, as St. Paul said [1 Cor. 11:24-26]: "You are to proclaim his death." For this reason, it is a frightening and horrifying task to be a bishop, pastor, or preacher today, for no one knows about this testament anymore, let alone that they are to preach it as their single highest duty and obligation. It will be difficult for them to account for so many souls who go to ruin because such preaching was lacking.

4. People should pray, but not in the customary way by turning pages in a prayer book or counting beads on the rosary.[77] Instead, we should bring particularly pressing needs [before God], earnestly seek aid, and place our faith and trust in God so intently that we have no doubt we will be heard. Saint Bernard told his [monastic] brothers this very thing: "Dear brethren, do not belittle your prayers as if they were said in vain; for in truth I tell you that before you utter the words they are already written down in heaven. And you should be quite certain that your prayer will be answered or, if not, that it was not in your best interest for it to be answered."[e]

77. Luther here calls into question traditional modes of praying. The rosary was a form of medieval devotion popularized by the Dominican Order. The "Hail Mary," the Lord's Prayer, the Gloria Patri, and other prayers were repeated in groups of ten that were tracked by fingering beads on a string or cord.

e   From a Lenten sermon, which Luther often cited, by Bernard of

Prayer is therefore a special exercise of faith, which consequently makes it so absolutely acceptable [to God], for either the prayer is answered directly or something better than what was requested is granted. As St. James says [1:6-8]: "Let whoever prays ask in faith, never doubting . . . for whoever doubts . . . does not expect to receive anything from God." That is a straightforward declaration that simultaneously promises and denies. All who do not believe receive nothing—neither what they asked for nor anything better.

In order to awaken such faith, Christ himself also said (in Mark 11[:24]): "I tell you, whatever you ask for, believe that you will receive it and it will certainly happen."[f] And in Luke 11[:9-13]: "Ask and it will be given you, search and you will find, knock and it will be opened for you. For whoever asks receives, whoever searches finds, and whoever knocks, for them it is opened. What father among you gives his son a stone when he asks for bread, or a snake when he asks for fish, or a scorpion when he asks for an egg? If you, then, who by nature are not good, know how to give good gifts to your children, how much more will your heavenly Father give a good spirit to all who ask."[g]

5. Who is so callous and hardhearted that such powerful words do not move such a person to pray joyously, gladly, and with complete trust? But think how many prayers would have to be rewritten if someone wanted to pray rightly according to these words! Every church and cloister is without question full of praying and singing. How, then, can it happen that they bring so little improvement or benefit and things keep getting worse? The reason can only be what St. James indicates [4:3]: "You pray much, but you receive nothing because you pray in the wrong way." For where this faith and trust are lacking in prayer, then it is dead and nothing

Clairvaux, a prominent Cistercian abbot, theologian, and churchman. See MPL 183:180. For the list of citations by Luther, see MLStA 2:45, n. 335.

f   Following the Latin Vulgate.

g   Luther follows the Vulgate, which read "good spirit." His translation of the New Testament from 1522 reads (with the Greek): "Holy Spirit."

but toil and effort; even if something is received, it is only useful in a temporal way, offering no benefits or help for souls but instead blinding them and causing them great harm. They go rattling on, without noticing whether or not they receive what they request or even desire or expect [an answer]; they remain obdurate in this unbelief, which is a deplorable habit that contradicts both the exercise of faith and the essence of prayer.

From this it follows that the individuals[h] who pray properly never doubt that their prayer is pleasing to God and heard, even if they do not receive exactly what they asked for. For in prayer one should lay all one's needs before God but never limit God to a certain amount, ways and means, place or purpose. Instead, if God wants to give something better or different from what we imagine, we should leave it to God's discretion, "for often we do not know what we ask," as St. Paul says in Rom. 8[:26], and, as he says in Eph. 3[:20], "God can do and give far more than we can grasp." Hence, as far as prayer goes, let there be no doubt that it is pleasing to God and is heard. But, still, let God choose the time and place, the amount and the purpose, let God make things turn out as they should. The ones who pray rightly "pray to God in spirit and truth."[i] For those who do not believe they will be heard sin against this commandment on the right side through their unbelief, wandering far from it. Those who place a limit on the answer to their prayer sin on the left side by wandering too close in testing God. Hence God has forbidden both things so that no one deviates from the commandment in either direction—either with unbelief or with testing God—but with pure faith stays on the right road, trusting God without any restrictions.

6. Thus, we see that this commandment, like the second, is nothing other than a matter of practicing and reflecting on the first commandment, which consists of faith, trust,

---

h   Singular in the original.

i   John 4:24. Luther here uses the terms *Anbeter* and *anbeten*, derived from the word "to pray" (*beten*), which could also be translated "adorer" and "adore."

confidence, hope, and love of God. And we see that the first commandment is the captain and that faith is the chief work and life of all other works, which cannot be good without it, as I said.

Now you may ask, "What if I cannot believe that my prayer will be heard and is pleasing to God?" Answer: this is why faith, prayer, and other good works are commanded, so that you might see what you can and cannot do. Then, when you find that you are unable to believe and act in this manner, you may humbly lament this before God and with a small spark of faith you may begin to strengthen it more and more each day by applying it through all of life in every action. For there is no one on earth who has not been afflicted with a weakness of faith (itself the first and highest commandment). In the gospels even the holy apostles—Peter most of all—were weak in faith so that they even begged Christ [Luke 17:5], "Lord, increase our faith!" And he frequently scolded them for having such little faith.

Do not, therefore, despair and throw up your hands if you discover that in prayer or other works you do not believe as strongly as you should and would like to believe. Instead, you should give thanks to God from the bottom of your heart that he has revealed your weakness to you and thereby teaches and admonishes you how necessary it is for you to practice your faith and strengthen it daily. Look at how many people go on praying, singing, reading [Masses], working, and appearing to be great saints, without ever coming to the realization about how it is going for them with faith, the chief work. In this way they blind themselves and lead others astray, imagining that everything is as it should be. Thus, they calmly build upon the sand of their own works[j] without any faith and not upon God's grace and promise with a sound and pure faith.

For this reason, as long as we live, however long that might be, we have our hands full with remaining pupils of the first commandment and of faith with all its works and troubles, never ceasing to learn. No one knows what it

j   See Matt. 7:26.

78. The "spiritual walks of life" included all clergy, monks, and nuns. The term *Fathers* was used for prominent Christians in the early church, especially some so-called Desert Fathers, that is, monks in Egypt, some of whom practiced continuous prayer.

means to trust God alone except the person who makes a beginning and tries to put it into practice.

7. Consider this. If no other good work were provided, would not prayer alone be enough to exercise faith for the entire span of human life? For this very reason, those in spiritual walks of life were pledged to this work. For example, in former times some Fathers prayed day and night.[78] Of course, no Christian has time to "pray without ceasing,"[k] but I am talking about spiritual prayer. That is, no one is so occupied by work that they cannot, if they wish, talk with God while working and place before him their own needs and the needs of others, beg and plead for help, and in so doing exercise and fortify their faith.

The Lord meant just that in Luke 18[:1], when he said to pray continuously without letting up, but at the same time in Matt. 6[:5-7] he forbade using many words and long prayers. In so doing he was chastising the hypocrites, not that he says that praying aloud for a long time is evil but that it is not the kind of true prayer that can happen at all times and that it is nothing without the inner prayer of faith. For we also have to practice outward prayer when appropriate, especially at Mass (as is also required by this commandment) and wherever it promotes inward prayer and faith—whether at home, in the fields, or during any kind of labor whatsoever. There is no time to say more about this here. It belongs to the exposition of the Lord's Prayer, in which all petitions and oral prayers are succinctly summarized.[l]

8. Where are the people who want to learn about and perform good works? Let them take up praying alone and practice it properly; then they will find that what the holy Fathers said is true: nothing is quite the work that prayer is.[m]

---

k   See 1 Thess. 5:17.

l   Luther is probably thinking of his 1519 *An Exposition of the Lord's Prayer for Simple Laypeople* (LW 42:15–81; WA 2:74–130). For another interpretation from 1519 (but also published in 1522), see his *Personal Prayer Book* (LW 43:3–35; WA 10/2:339–406). Later expositions include the *Large Catechism*, "The Lord's Prayer" (BC, 440–56; from 1529), and *A Simple Way to Pray* (LW 43:189–211; from 1535).

m   Luther is citing the *Vitae Patrum* (*Lives of the [Desert] Fathers*) V.12.1, a saying of Agathon (MPL 73:941).

Murmuring orally is easy or thought to be easy, but to accompany the words with authentic devotion and heartfelt earnestness, that is, with yearning and faith so that the heart truly desires what the words say and does not doubt they will be heard—that is a remarkable deed in God's eyes.

The evil spirit, however, opposes prayer with all its might. O how often it takes away the desire to pray by allowing no time and place for it or awakens so much doubt about whether a person is worthy to ask something of a majestic figure like God. It sows confusion until people themselves do not know whether it is important to pray or not, whether or not their prayers are pleasing to God, and many other fanciful thoughts. For the evil spirit fully appreciates how mighty each person's faith-filled prayers are, how much damage they inflict on that very spirit, and how useful they are for everyone. Consequently, it tries at all costs to stifle such prayer. Thus, people[n] must be truly wise and firmly hold that they and their prayers are not worthy before such an immense Majesty, in no way relying on their own worthiness nor letting their unworthiness prevent them from praying. But instead, they must look to God's commandment, hold it up to the devil, and declare: "Nothing is instigated because of my worthiness and nothing is prevented because of my unworthiness. I pray and act only because God, solely out of divine goodness, has promised to grant a hearing and grace to every unworthy person—and not only promised but also strictly, at the risk of earning his eternal anger and wrath, commanded me to pray, to trust, and to receive. Since it was not too much for the high Majesty to obligate in such a invaluable way his small unworthy worms to pray, to believe and to receive from him, would it be too much for me to accept this commandment joyfully, no matter how worthy or unworthy I might be?" This is how one must cast out the devil's insinuations—with God's command. Only then will he cease—otherwise never.

9. What hardships and other matters must a person present and lament before the almighty God in prayer in order

---

[n]　Singular in the original.

to exercise faith? Answer: first, one's own pressing hardships and afflictions. David says in Ps. 32[:7]: "You are my refuge amid the anguish that surrounds me and my assurance that I will be saved from all the evil round about." And in Ps. 142[:1-2]: "With my voice I appeal to God and with my mouth I implore the Lord. I will spread out my prayer before his countenance and pour out before him everything that oppresses me." Therefore, in the Mass a Christian should take up what seems lacking or is too much to bear and pour it out openly before God with tears and groans, as pitiably as possible, just as to a faithful father who is ready to help. If you are not aware of what you need or experience no attacks, then you should realize you could not be worse off. For the greatest attack occurs when you are so obdurate, hard-hearted, and insensitive as to be oblivious to any attacks.[o]

There is no better mirror for seeing what you need than the Decalogue, in which you discover what you lack and what you should seek. If, then, you find yourself with a weak faith, little hope, and scant love of God, or, alternatively if you find that you do not honor and praise God but, desiring your own honor and reputation instead, you prefer above everything else the approval of others, or, again, if you would rather not attend Mass or listen to the sermon or are too lazy to pray—in these matters no one is without failings—you should take these shortcomings more seriously than damage to your property, your body, or your honor. They are worse than any fatal disease, worse even than death itself. Next, you should earnestly lay these things before God, cry out to him, ask for help, and with complete confidence expect that you have been heard and that you will receive both help and mercy. Then go on to the second table of the commandments and discover how disobedient you have been, and still are, toward parents and others in authority; with how much anger and hatred you have verbally abused your neighbors;

o See sec. 25 above, under "The Second Good Work": "The most pernicious kind comes when there is no attack at all and everything is running smoothly." See also WA 50:272, where Luther refers to a sermon on the Song of Songs by Bernard of Clairvaux, XXXIII.16 (MPL 183:959).

and how you have attacked your neighbor with unchastity, avarice, and injustice in word and deed. Then you will see without a doubt that you are full of needs and misery and have reason enough to cry tears of blood, if you could.

10. I know full well that many people are so foolish that they will not ask for such things unless they see themselves as pure beforehand, thinking that God hears no one who remains in sin. All false preachers do this by not being devoted to faith and trust in God but emphasizing instead teachings about one's own works.

Consider this, you poor soul: if you have broken a leg or fallen into mortal danger, then you call on God, invoke this or that saint, and keep at it until your leg is healed and the danger is past. Now, you are not so foolish as to think that God listens to no one who has broken a leg or is in mortal danger. Indeed, you assume that God must listen to you even more if you are in severe distress and anguish. So, why, then, are you so foolish in the face of incomparably greater need and eternal harm? And so do you refuse to ask all the more for faith, hope, love, humility, obedience, chastity, gentleness, peace, and righteousness, as if you had no unbelief, doubt, arrogance, disobedience, anger, avarice, or unrighteousness whatsoever? Instead, the more you find yourselves lacking in all these things the more fervently and diligently you should pray and cry out for them.

We are so blind that we run to God with physical ailments and needs, but for illnesses of the soul we run away from God and are determined not to return until we are cured—as if there were two gods, one to help the body and one to aid the soul, or as if we ourselves could take care of spiritual needs, although they are greater than the physical. This is really a devilish bit of advice and counsel.

No, my dear! If you want to be cured of your sin, you must not pull back from God but run to him with more confidence than ever, entreating him as if you had suddenly been struck with some physical malady. God is not the enemy of sinners except for unbelievers, that is, for those who do not acknowledge and rue their sins or ask God for help. Instead, they want to cleanse themselves in advance by their presumption, to admit no need of divine grace, and do not allow God to be God, who gives to everyone and takes nothing in return.

11. The preceding pertains to prayer for personal needs in general.[p] The kind of prayer, however, that actually belongs to this commandment and is designated a work of the Sabbath is much better and more significant and should be offered for the assembly of all Christians, for the needs of all people, enemies and friends, and especially for those who reside in one's own parish or diocese. Saint Paul wrote to his disciple Timothy [1 Tim. 2:1-3]: "I charge you to make sure that prayer and supplication is made for everyone, for kings and all rulers, so that we can lead a quiet and peaceable life in the service of God and with integrity. For that is good and pleasing to God our Savior." Likewise, Jeremiah (in chapter 29[:7]) ordered the people of Israel to pray for the city and the land of Babylon, because "the peace of the city is your peace." Bar. 1[:11-12] states: "Pray for the life of the king of Babylon and for the life of his son, so that we may live in peace under their rule."[q]

This common prayer is precious and most powerful. It is the reason we gather. On this basis, moreover, the church is called a house of prayer,[r] so that we likewise, as one, should gather up our needs and the needs of all people and bring them before God, appealing for grace. It must be done, however, with deep feeling and earnestness, so that the needs of all penetrate our hearts and, while actually suffering with them, we pray for them in faith and trust. If that kind of prayer is not offered during the Mass, it is better to have no Mass at all. For how does this square with coming together bodily in a house of prayer—given that the act of gathering itself shows we ought to pray in common for the whole community—if we scatter the prayers and divide them up so that each person prays only for personal needs and no one bothers with or cares for the needs of anybody else? How

p   Sections 9–10.
q   The book of Baruch in the Apocrypha is written as a letter from Baruch, Jeremiah's secretary, to the people and priests of Jerusalem.
r   See Luke 19:46.

then is it possible for prayer to be beneficial, good, pleasing, and "in common," or a work of "the Sabbath" or "of the assembly,"[79] if people say only their private little prayers—one for this, another for that—and have nothing but self-serving and self-seeking prayers to which God is averse?

12. An expression of common prayer has remained in use for a long time—when, after the sermon, one recites the confession of sin and prays for all of Christendom from the pulpit. But that should not suffice as is now the custom and practice. Instead, it should become an admonition to offer prayer throughout the Mass for these needs, to which the preacher urges us and, so that we may pray in a worthy manner, reminds us of our sin and humbles us. But this should be done as briefly as possible so that the people together as one community may lament their sin before God and pray for everyone with sincerity and faith.

Would God that every group would attend Mass and pray in this way so that together the earnest, heartfelt cry of all the people would ascend to God. Think what immeasurable value and support would result from such prayer! What could confront all evil spirits more menacingly? How could there be here on earth any greater work that would sustain so many upright people and convert so many sinners?

In truth, the Christian church on earth possesses no greater force or work than such common prayer to counter everything that harasses it. The evil spirit knows this quite well and does everything it can to hinder this prayer. It lets us build pretty churches, create numerous endowments, play instruments, read and sing, celebrate many Masses, and promote unlimited pomp. It has no regrets about this but even encourages us to imagine such things are the finest and to think that with them we have done everything just right. When prayer that is communal, strong, and effective dies out, such hypocrisy smothers it. Where prayer is covered over, no one can diminish that spirit or defeat it. But when it sees that we do want to engage in this prayer, whether it happens in a thatched cottage or a pigsty, the evil spirit cannot ignore it but has more fear of that sty than of any tall, beautiful churches whatsoever, with their steeples and bells,

79. The "common prayers" labeled the general prayers of the assembled congregation. Luther is asking how they can be called common, shared prayers when no one shares them.

A man with a sword holds a rosary.
Published in Luther's
Sermon on Saint Michael, 1522.

80. At private confession, the priest would often assign the penitent a certain number of prayers like the Our Father and the Ave Maria to be said as penance. The rosary helped a person keep track of the number of times these prayers were recited.

in which such prayer is not present. The places and buildings in which we assemble do not matter, but rather only this invincible prayer that we truly offer in common and lift up to God.

13. We observe the effectiveness of this prayer in Abraham, when he prayed long ago for the five cities, Sodom, Gomorrah, and so on, and eventually convinced God not to destroy them if ten godly persons—two in each city—could be found.[s] Think what could happen if many people in a congregation appealed to God with sincere and heartfelt trust! James writes: "Beloved, pray for one another that you may be saved. For the prayer of godly persons can do very much if it is constant and does not let up"[t] (that is, does not cease asking God—as many irresolute people do—even if they do not immediately receive that for which they are praying). James uses Elijah as an example [James 5:17-18]: "He was a human being like us and prayed that it might not rain, and for three years and six months it did not rain. Then he prayed again and it rained, and everything bore fruit." Many utterances and examples in Scripture encourage us to pray, but always in earnest and with faith, as David says: "God's eyes look upon the devout, and his ears listen to their prayers."[u] Likewise [Ps. 145:18]: "God is near to all those who call upon him, to all who call upon him in truth." Why does the psalmist add "in truth"? Because it is not praying or calling upon God when only the mouth mumbles.

What is God supposed to do when you come to church with your mouth, a prayer book, and a rosary and set your mind on nothing other than getting through the words the prescribed number of times?[80] If someone asks you, however, what the point was or what you intended to pray for, you will have no idea because it has not occurred to you to place this or that concern before God or to ask for anything. Your only reason for praying is because so many prayers have been prescribed for you, which you now want to perform and get

s   Gen. 18:22-33.

t   James 5:16 from the Latin Vulgate.

u   Combining Ps. 33:18 with 39:12 in the Vulgate.

through. Is it any wonder, then, that thunder and lightning so often set church buildings on fire, since we turn houses of prayer into houses of ridicule by calling this prayer, when we ask for nothing and bring no concerns to God? When we pray, we should behave like those who bring petitions to powerful princes. Such petitioners do not intend to run on at the mouth; otherwise, the prince would think they were crazy or making fun of him. On the contrary, they plan out precisely what they are going to say and present their request with great care while at the same time committing it to his gracious favor, confident that the petition will be heard. Likewise, we must talk with God about specific matters, identify some pressing needs by name, entrust it to his grace and goodwill and not doubt that it will be heard. God has promised to hear such prayers, and that is more than any earthly lord has promised.

14. We are masters of this way of praying: when we suffer from illness or other bodily afflictions, then we invoke St. Christopher[81] and St. Barbara,[82] or we vow to make a pilgrimage to St. James or to go here and there.[v] In such cases, we discover earnest imploring and absolute confidence, that is, everything that belongs to proper prayer. But when we attend Mass in church, we stand there like statues[w] and can think of nothing to ask or nothing to lament. The rosary beads clack, the prayer book rustles, and the mouth babbles, but nothing more than that.

The martyrdom of St. Barbara.

81. A completely legendary figure who was included among the fourteen auxiliary saints, or "holy helpers," Christopher first became popular when the bubonic plague swept Germany in the fourteenth century. He was allegedly a martyr during the third century. As "Christ-bearer" (the meaning of his Greek name), legend had it that this giant could not carry the Christ child across a stream he controlled. Still known today as the patron of travelers, in the Middle Ages he was also invoked against epilepsy and plague.

82. Also one of the "holy helpers," Barbara, whose name first appeared in the seventh century, supposedly

---

v   See p. 272 above.

w   German: *Ölgötzen* (oil gods), people who stand there rigid without saying anything; derived from oil paintings of saints and perhaps connected to Peter sleeping on the Mount of Olives (Matt. 26:30, 40-46).

suffered martyrdom in the third or fourth century after being handed over to Roman authorities by her pagan father; her aid was sought against perils of storms and fire. Legend had it that people who prayed at her grave were healed of their diseases.

St. Christopher carrying
Christ across a stream.

If you ask what you should request and lament in prayer, the Ten Commandments and the Lord's Prayer will easily teach you. Open your eyes wide and look hard at your life and all the lives in the whole Christian church,[x] especially those in the spiritual walk of life,[y] and you will find that faith, hope, love, obedience, chastity, and other virtues are trampled underfoot and that all kinds of horrible vices prevail. You will also see that good preachers and religious leaders are scarce and that knaves, children, fools, and women are in control so that, given this terrible anger of God, it is imperative all over the world to pray nonstop with nothing but tears of blood. It is all too true that never before has it been so necessary to pray as from now until the world ends. If these awful afflictions do not move you to wailing and lamenting, do not let your spiritual walk of life, your [monastic] orders, your good works, or your prayers deceive you. There is not a Christian muscle or quality in you, however pious you may be. This was all prophesied: that at the very time God's anger is hottest and the distress of Christendom at its worst, no one can be found who will cry out to God and make intercession. Thus Isaiah laments in chapter 64[:5, 7]: "You are angry with us, but there is no one to stand up and hold you back." Likewise, Ezek. 22[:30-31] states: "And I sought for anyone among them who would repair the wall and stand in the breach before me; but I found no one. Therefore I have poured out my anger upon them and devoured them in the blaze of my wrath." With these words, God shows how he wants us to stand before him and protect one another from his wrath, just as is often written about the prophet Moses that he restrained God from pouring out his anger upon the people of Israel.[z]

15. What will become of those who not only ignore the harm done to the whole Christian church and say no prayers

---

x   Here and in pars. 15–16, the German is *Christenheit*, literally, "Christianity" or "Christendom." It is Luther's term for the entirety of the Christian church.

y   See p. 310, n. 78.

z   Exod. 32:11-14; Num. 14:13-19; 21:7-9; Ps. 106:23.

for it but instead even laugh and take delight in passing judgment on their neighbors' sins and gossiping about them in the worst way? And yet, without fear or shame, they attend church, hear the Mass, say prayers, and see themselves and want to be seen as godly Christians. They need to be prayed for twice over, while we need pray only once for those whom they judge, slander, and ridicule. That such people would exist was presaged by the crucified thief on Christ's left hand, who blasphemed Christ in his suffering, pain, and misery, and by all those who likewise reviled Christ on the cross when they should have been helping him.[a]

My God, how blind, how mad we Christians have become! When, heavenly Father, will this anger cease? That we make fun of, curse, and judge the sorry state of Christendom, which we gather in the church and at Mass to pray for, comes from our stupid minds. When the Turks devastate towns and the countryside with their inhabitants and destroy churches,[83] we think immediately that huge damage has been done to Christendom. We complain and force kings and the princes into battle. When, however, faith disappears, love becomes cold, God's word is neglected, and all kinds of sins gain the upper hand, no one steps forth to fight them. Even though pope, bishops, and priests ought to join the spiritual battle as generals,[b] captains, and commanders against this far worse spiritual "Turk." They are themselves this "Turk" and the princes and leaders of the devil's army, just as Judas was for the Jews when they arrested Christ.[c] To initiate the process of putting Jesus to death, it took one of the best: an apostle, bishop, and priest. In the same manner, Christendom must be brought to ruin by those who should be guarding it. They remain so deluded, however, that they want to devour the Turk while they set their own houses and sheepfolds on fire and let them burn along with the sheep and everything in them. Nonetheless, they are still worried

83. The Muslim Ottoman Empire and its troops, called by Luther the "Turks," threatened central Europe in the 1520s and 1540s. Belgrade and much of Hungary fell to the invading armies in 1521.

a   Luke 23:35-39.

b   German: *Herzogen*, usually translated "dukes," but here taken literally, "those who lead an army."

c   Matt. 26:47-50.

about the wolf in the bush. This is our sentence; this is our reward for the ingratitude we have shown for the endless grace that Christ has freely acquired for us with his precious blood, his arduous labor, and his bitter death.

16. Now where are the idlers who do not know how to do good works? Where are those who run to Rome and St. James [of Compostela], to this place or another? Take only the work connected with the Mass as your own. Look at the sins and failures of your neighbors, have pity on them, let yourself be moved to cry out to God and pray for them. Do the same for all the hardships we suffer throughout Christendom, particularly for its rulers whom God allows to be seduced and fall so woefully—to the unbearable punishment and plague of us all. If you do that consistently, be assured that you are one of the best soldiers and commanders not only against the Turks but also against the devil and the powers of hell. And if you do not do this, how would it help you even if you performed every miracle of all the saints, or strangled all the Turks and yet were found guilty of not having heeded the needs of your neighbor and therefore having sinned against love? On the last day, Christ will not ask how often you prayed for yourself, fasted, made a pilgrimage, and did this or that, but how often you did something good for others, especially for the least of all.[d] Among the least are also those who live in sins, spiritual poverty, captivity, and need who are far more numerous than those who suffer from physical maladies. Watch out, therefore, because our self-chosen good works lead us back into ourselves, so that we seek only our own benefit and blessedness. But God's commandments force us to our neighbors, so that we only benefit them and their blessedness. Just as Christ on the cross prayed not for himself alone but rather for us when he said [Luke 23:34]: "Father, forgive them, for they know not what they are doing," so we must also pray for one another. Everyone is able to see from this how perverted and reprehensible people are who slander, despise, and brazenly judge others; they do nothing but revile those for whom they should be

d   Matt. 25:31-46.

praying. No one is more deeply immersed in these vices than those who for the sake of their beautiful, sparkling selves do many and various good works of their own merely in order to outshine others and gain their approval.

17. The spiritual meaning of this commandment[84] contains an even greater work that encompasses human nature in its entirety. Here one has to realize that in Hebrew *sabbath* means "cease working"[e] or "rest," because (Gen. 2[:2]) "on the seventh day God rested from all the works that he had done." For this reason, God also commanded us to rest on the seventh day and refrain from the works that we have been doing the other six days. For us, this very Sabbath has been transformed into Sunday, and the other days are called workdays, but Sunday is called a day of rest or a feast day or a holy day. Would God that there were in Christendom no feast days except Sunday and that the feast days of Our Lady[85] and of the saints were all moved to Sundays. As a consequence, by laboring on workdays, many more vices would be avoided, and the land would not be so poor and devastated.

This rest or cessation of works is twofold: bodily and spiritual; hence, the commandment must be understood in two ways. Physical refraining from work and resting were addressed earlier: we stop the work of our hands and our labor in order to assemble in church, be present at Mass, listen to God's word, and pray communally and with one accord. To be sure, this rest is physical and not commanded by God for the Christian church, as the apostle says in Col. 2[:16-17]: "Let no one obligate you . . . to observe any feast day . . . for these were only prefiguring of what is to come." Now, however, truth has been fulfilled so that every day is a feast day of rest, as Isa. 66[:23] says: "One feast day will follow the next," and every day will be free from work.[f] Nonetheless, such a rest day is necessary and has been set up by the whole Christian church for the sake of those not under a

84. Luther uses spiritual or "allegorical" interpretations of Scripture throughout his career, borrowing insights from the ancient and medieval traditions and using them to emphasize faith's dependence on God's word. This is his second main point regarding this commandment. See above, p. 303.

85. Mary, the mother of Jesus. When feasts of Mary and the saints fell on weekdays, work was stopped in favor of special Masses and processions.

e German: *feyr*. This word means both rest and, in a transferred meaning, "festival" or "feast."

f German: *werckel tag*, a day of little or no work or chores.

86. Literally, "the imperfect ones." Medieval theologians distinguished between believers in a state of grace and those under a vow who were said to be in a state of perfection, not that they were themselves perfect but rather that they were in a place where their good works were more valuable for reaching the goal of perfection before God.

87. The so-called Divine Office, or times of prayer at intervals throughout the day, was observed in cloisters and chapters of clergy as Matins, Lauds, Terce, Sext, None, Vespers, and Compline. The Divine Office provided for the entire Psalter to be recited each week.

vow[86] and working folk so that they have time to come and hear the word of God. For, as we see, priests and monks say the Mass every day, pray the hours,[87] and exercise themselves in the word of God by studying, reading, and hearing it read. For that reason, they are, over and above others, exempted from work, supported by regular incomes, have a day of rest every day and perform the works of Sabbath every day. They have no days for small chores, and one day is like another. If all of us were perfect and well versed in the gospel, then we could work every day if we wished or have a day of rest whenever we could. For now such rest is not necessary or commanded except to learn God's word and to pray.

Spiritual rest, for which above all else God intended this commandment, entails not only laying down our work and labor but—much more—letting God alone work in us without applying any power of our own at all. How does that take place? As follows: Humankind, damaged by sin, has an inordinate love and predilection for all things sinful. As Scripture says in Gen. 8[:21], "The human heart and mind always aspire to evil," that is, to arrogance, disobedience, anger, hate, avarice, unchastity, and so on. To sum it up: in all that individuals do or leave undone they seek their own will, advantage, and honor more than that of God or the neighbor. All their works, words, and thoughts, even their entire lives, are evil and not godly.

If God is to work and live in them, all these vices and corruption must be strangled and stamped out so that a rest and ceasing of all our works, words, thoughts, and lives may take place—so that from now on, as Paul says in Gal. 2[:20], "not we, but Christ lives in us," acts and speaks. This does not happen in the midst of sweet and pleasant days; instead, here one must inflict pain on human nature and suffer such pain. Now comes the conflict between spirit and flesh,[g] with the spirit resisting anger, lust, and pride while the flesh prefers lasciviousness, honor, and security. Thus, Paul says in Gal. 5[:24]: "Those who belong to our Lord Christ have crucified their flesh with its vices and desires." Here is the source

g See Gal. 5:16-17.

of good works like fasting, keeping vigils, and performing strenuous labors,[88] about which some people talk and write a great deal, although they are unaware of their origin and purpose. Hence we will say a few things about them.

18. This kind of rest, in which our working ceases and God alone works in us, happens in two ways: first, through our own practice and, second, through the external practice and pressure from others.[h] Our own practice should be done and ordered as follows. First, we observe where our flesh, senses, will, and thoughts are inciting us and then resist them and not follow them, as the wise man says in Sir. [18:30]: "Do not follow your base desires." Likewise, Deut. 12[:8]: "Do not do . . . what appears right to you."[i]

Every day a person must use the prayers said by David [Ps. 119:35, 37]: "Lord, guide me onto your path . . . and prevent me from going my own way," and many similar utterances, all of which can be summarized in one petition: "Your kingdom come to us."[j] So many base desires exist in such great variety and the leading of the evil one is so clever, polished, and appealing that individuals[k] are unable to control themselves and stay on the straight and narrow. They must let go and entrust themselves to God's rule, relying in no way on their reason. As Jeremiah says [10:23]: "I know, O LORD, that the way of human beings is not in their control." This was manifested when the children of Israel departed from Egypt through a wilderness where there was no road, no food, no drink, and no aid. Therefore, "God went ahead of them by day in a pillar of cloud and by night in a pillar of fire," fed them from heaven with heavenly bread, and prevented their clothes and their shoes from wearing out, as we read in the books of Moses.[l] Thus we pray, "'Your kingdom come,' so that you, God, rule over us and not we ourselves." Nothing is more dangerous than our own reason and will. This is the

88. "Vigils" involved staying awake in prayer and meditation, especially on the eve of a festival. "Labors" were associated with monastic practice of "prayer and labor" (*ora et labora*) and were also understood as penitential.

h   For this second kind of rest, see below, par. 22.
i   Rendered in line with the Vulgate.
j   From the Lord's Prayer (Matt. 6:10; Luke 11:2).
k   Singular in the original.
l   See Exod. 13:21; 16:4; and Deut. 29:5.

first and best work of God in us and the best practice for letting go of our works: to shut down our reason and will, to rest and entrust oneself to God in all things, especially when these works appear to be spiritual and good.

19. Discipline of the flesh follows from this: practices for slaying its coarse, evil desires and creating rest and repose. We must put the flesh to death and quiet it with fasting, vigils, or labors; and for that reason, we are teaching why and to what extent we should fast, perform vigils, or labor.

Unfortunately, there are many blind people who practice chastising themselves, whether through fasting, vigils, or labor, only because they imagine that these things are good works through which they may merit a great deal. They dive in and at times so overtax themselves that they wreck their bodies and drive themselves mad. Those people are even blinder who rate their fasting not according to how little they eat or how long they refrain from eating but by the kind of food from which they abstain. Fasting is worth more, they believe, if they eat no meat, butter, or eggs. Above these are those who try to fast like the saints and choose certain days like Wednesday, or Saturday, or the feast days of St. Barbara and St. Sebastian, and the like.[89] In such fasting, all of these folk seek only the work itself and, when they have accomplished this, assume they have done well. I will not mention those who fast and yet get completely drunk or those who "fast" by eating so much fish and other foods that they approximate genuine fasting and preserve its benefits as much as if consuming meat, butter, and eggs instead. That kind of "fasting" is not fasting at all but rather a mockery of fasting and of God.

Therefore, I would permit individuals to select for themselves certain days, specific foods, or the extent of their fasts as they wish, as long as they do not restrict it to the activity but take into consideration their own "flesh." They should correlate the extent of their fasting, vigils, and other labors with the degree to which their flesh is lustful and arrogant and no more, in spite of what the pope, the church, a bishop, a father confessor, or whoever may have commanded. For the extent of fasting, vigils or labors should not be measured

89. The Feast of St. Barbara (December 4) was often designated as a special fast day during Advent, and the Feast of St. Sebastian (January 20), who according to legend was martyred by being tied to a tree and shot with arrows, was celebrated as the day when the sap returned to the trees and, hence, a day for eating fruit.

by the specific foods, days, or amount but by the increase or decrease of carnal lust and arrogance. Damping down and slaying those vices is the only reason that fasting, vigils, and labors were instituted. If those vices did not exist, then eating would be as good as fasting, sleeping as good as vigils, and leisure as good as labors. One would be as good as another—without distinction.

20. Suppose someone discovers that fish causes more arrogance in the flesh than eggs or meat, then that person should eat meat instead of fish. Or again, if fasting drives someone mad or ruins the stomach or body, or is unnecessary for slaying the flesh's arrogance, then that person should omit it entirely and eat, sleep, and relax as much as it takes to stay healthy, even if it contradicts the precepts of the church and the rules of religious orders and societies.[90] For no precept of the church and no rule of a religious order can set a higher standard for fasting, vigils, or labor or demand more observance than it takes to tame or slay the flesh and its desires. Where this goal is exceeded and fasting, eating, sleeping, and keeping vigils either demand more than the flesh can bear or than is necessary to slay lust or ruin the body and crush the mind, no one would think that a person has done a good work or can appeal to the church's precepts or other regulations as an excuse.[91] People will think such persons[m] are guilty of self-neglect or have as much as become their own murderers. The human body was not created for killing its life and natural functions but only for slaying its arrogance. Even were that arrogance so strong and mighty that it could not be adequately resisted without ruining and damaging bodily life, still, as I said, in fasting, keeping vigils, and laboring, attention should not be fixed on the activities themselves—neither the days, nor the amount, nor the kind of food—but on the arrogant and lustful Adam[92] in order to ward off its cravings.

21. On this basis we can evaluate how wisely or foolishly some women act when they are pregnant and how a person should behave toward sick people. Women who foolishly

90. In addition to orders of monks and friars, in the late Middle Ages guilds and other groups of laypeople formed themselves into religious confraternities with a variety of religious duties.

91. Limiting fasting for health reasons was a standard part of medieval pastoral advice.

92. That is, the Old Creature, mired in sin and self-worship.

m Singular in the original.

insist on fasting would rather risk great danger to themselves and their fetuses than to forgo fasting with other people. They make something a matter of conscience where there is none, and where they should follow their conscience they do not." It is all the fault of the preachers who carry on about fasting without clarifying its correct use, extent, fruits, cause, or goal. For the same reason, people who are sick should be allowed to eat and drink every day as much as they wish. In short: once the arrogance of the flesh has come to an end, every reason for fasting vigils, labor, eating only this or that has already ended, too, and no binding commandment exists any longer.

At the same time, a person should not let a careless laziness about slaying the flesh's arrogance emerge from this freedom. The wily [old] Adam has many tricks by which to find a way to pretend that the head or body is being ruined. So some people seize on this and say that it is neither necessary nor obligatory to fast or chastise themselves and that they can eat any food they want—as if they had been diligently practiced fasting for a long time when in fact they have never tried it.

We should be no less cautious, however, about giving offense to those who are inadequately informed and consider it a grave sin if someone else does not fast or eat the same way they do. In this case, one should patiently instruct them and not simply despise them openly or spite them by consuming this or that food, but instead show them the cause for doing this and lead them with forbearance to the same insight. If, however, they are too stubborn and refuse to listen, let them go their own way while we do what we know is right.*

22. The second practice* arises when others attack us, namely, when we are harmed by other people or by devils that take our property and our honor, make our bodies ill, and in every possible way drive us to anger, impatience, and

---

n   That is, they strictly kept fasting, instead of caring for the safety of themselves or their child.

o   Luther will express this same concern for the weak in his so-called Invocavit Sermons of March 1522 (LW 51:71–73).

p   For the first practice, see par. 18 above.

unrest. For God's work reigns in us according to God's wisdom, not our reason, and according to God's purity and virtue, not the arrogance of our flesh. For God's work is wisdom and purity; our work is foolishness and impurity—and they should cease. Thus, God's work should reign in us according to God's peace and not our anger, impatience, and turmoil. Peace is also God's work; impatience is the work of our flesh that should cease and die, so that we may keep in every respect a spiritual Sabbath, stopping our own activity and letting God work in us.

In order to put to death our works and the [old] Adam, God hangs around our necks many unpleasant burdens that make us angry, much suffering that tries our patience, and finally death and the world's contempt. By doing these things, God is simply trying to expunge our anger, impatience, and turmoil and replace them with his work, that is, with his peace. As Isaiah says in chapter 28: "God undertakes a strange work" in order to arrive at his proper work.[93][q] What does this mean? He means that God sends us suffering and turmoil in order to teach us patience and peace. God permits us to die in order to make us alive until each person is so peaceful and quiet that it does not matter whether things go well or poorly, whether one lives or dies, is honored or dishonored. At that point, God alone dwells there and human works are no more. This is what it means to keep the Sabbath rest and make it holy in the right way. Here there is no human control, delight, or sorrow at all. Instead, God alone leads each human being, and nothing is present but divine delight, joy, and peace along with all the other works and virtues.

23. God esteems these works so highly that he commands us not only to observe the Sabbath but also to make or "keep it holy."[94] In this way, God indicates that nothing is more precious than suffering, dying, and misfortune; for they are sacred and make individuals holy by leading them away from

93. This notion of God's alien and proper work, related to the distinction between law and gospel, is also tied to Isaiah 28 by Philip Melanchthon (1497–1560) in the *Apology of the Augsburg Confession*, XII.51–54 (BC, 195). See also the *Heidelberg Disputation*, above, p. 90.

94. Luther now turns to explaining the second half of the commandment, "and keep it holy." See Exod. 20:8 and Deut. 5:12.

q   Isa. 28:21: "For the Lord will rise up as on Mount Perazim, he will rage as in the valley of Gibeon to do his deed—strange is his deed!—and to work his work—alien is his work!"

their works to God's work in the same way that dedicating a church turns a regular building into a house of worship. Likewise, people should regard suffering and misfortune as holy things, and be glad and thank God when they strike. For when they come, they make people holy so that they may fulfill this commandment, be saved and redeemed from their sinful works. Thus David says [Ps. 116:15]: "The death of his holy ones is precious in his sight."

To strengthen us, God not only commanded us to rest—for nature does not like to suffer and die so that it is a bitter day of rest when its works become useless and dead—but God also comforted us with many words from Scripture, as it says in Ps. 91[:15]: "I am with them in all their suffering and will rescue them," and Ps. 34[:18]: "The Lord is near to all who suffer and will help them."

Since not even that was enough, God provided a convincing example, his dearest and only Son, Jesus Christ, our Lord. On that Sabbath, an entire day of rest,[95] he lay in the grave divested of all his works and became the first to fulfill this commandment, although he did not need it for himself. He did it to comfort us, so that in suffering and dying we could be still and at peace. Given that Christ was raised after his Sabbath rest and from that point on lived only in God and God in him, so also, through slaying our [old] Adam (which is completed only after the death and burial of the body), we are raised into God, so that God lives and works in us eternally. Look! There are three sides of human nature—reason, desire, and aversion—into which all human works may be classified. They must be choked out by these three practices: God's rule, self-discipline, and suffering inflicted by others. Then we can take our rest spiritually in God and leave God room to do his work.

24.[96] These actions and suffering should take place in faith and in confident expectation of divine succor so that all works stay rooted in the first commandment and in faith, as we said above, and faith is exercised and strengthened in those actions. All the other commandments and works are set up for the sake of faith. Notice how a beautiful golden ring is made from the first three commandments and how

95. Holy Saturday between Good Friday and the first Easter.

96. The following summarizes Luther's interpretation of the first three commandments and their relation to faith.

the second commandment flows into the third from the first commandment and faith, and likewise the third commandment runs through the second and into the first. For the first work is faith: having a good heart and trusting in God, from which flows the second good work: praising God's name, acknowledging God's grace, and giving honor to God alone. After that comes the third work: worshiping God by praying, attending to the sermon, and contemplating and meditating on God's blessings, then by chastising and subjugating the flesh.

When the evil spirit notices such faith, honor, and worship of God, it goes on a rampage and starts persecution. It attacks our body, property, reputation, and life, and brings down upon us illness, poverty, shame, and death—all of which God has preordained and imposed on us for our own good.[97] Note that with this begins the other work or rest of the third commandment, in which faith "is severely tested like gold in the fire."[r] It is a remarkable thing to keep on trusting in God, although God brings death, disgrace, sickness, and poverty, and to maintain that God is still the kindest Father of all when faced with such a cruel example of wrath. But that must happen regarding this work of the third commandment. Suffering forces faith to call upon and praise God's name during the suffering. In this way, the third commandment again returns to the second commandment, and through the invocation and praise of God's name faith grows and comes into its own, and it becomes stronger through these two works of the second and the third commandments. So faith goes forth into those works and through those works returns to itself, just as "the sun rises until its setting and then returns to the place of its rising."[s] In Scripture, the daytime is dedicated to the peaceful life with works and the night to the suffering life with adversity. Faith, however, lives and is active in both, "goes in and out," as Christ says in John [10:9].[t]

97. Here Luther reframes the evil intent of bodily injury caused by persecution into a tool of God for discipline. Luther may even have his own attacks in mind.

r   Sir. 2:5.

s   Ps. 19:6, reading with the Vulgate.

t   Both the German and Latin texts have John 6. But see John 10:9: "[they] will come in and go out and find pasture."

25. In the Lord's Prayer, we offer petitions according to this order of good works in the commandments. First we say, "Our Father in heaven," words of the first work, faith, which, according to the first commandment, does not doubt that it has a merciful God and Father in heaven. Second, "Hallowed be your name," through which faith desires God's name, honor, and glory to be praised and calls upon God's name in all times of need, as the second commandment says. Third, "Your kingdom come," in which we ask for the true Sabbath and day of rest, for our works to cease and for God's work alone to be in us and for God to reign in us as in his own kingdom, as he himself says [Luke 17:21]: "See, the kingdom of God is nowhere but in you yourselves." In the fourth part, "Your will be done," we ask that we may obey the seven commandments of the second table and hold fast to them. Faith is also exercised in their works, which are directed toward the neighbor, just as it is exercised in the works of the first three commandments, which are directed toward God. The first three petitions of the Lord's Prayer contain the words "you" and "your" so that these petitions seek only what belongs to God. The other petitions all say "us" and "our," because in them we are asking for things that are good for us and for our salvation. All we have recounted up to now pertains to the first table of Moses and has painted the noblest good works in broad strokes for the simple folk. Now comes the second table.

The First Commandment
of the Second Table of Moses[98]

"Honor your father and mother." [u]

From this commandment we learn that after the noble works required by the first three commandments there is no greater work than to obey and serve those whom God has appointed as authorities over us. For this reason, dis-

98. Commandments 4–10. See also above, p. 303, n. 66.

u Exod. 20:12; Deut. 5:16.

obedience is even worse than murder, unchastity, theft, dishonesty, and anything else covered by the last six commandments. For making distinctions among sins—which ones are more serious than others—can be difficult for us to recognize except by observing the order of God's commandments, even though there is also a distinction among the works within each commandment. For who does not know that cursing is worse than being angry, killing worse than cursing, killing father and mother worse than killing just anyone? These seven commandments teach us how we ought to practice good works toward others and, first of all, toward those placed over us.

1. **The first work** of this commandment is to honor our biological fathers and mothers. This honor does not only consist in outward gestures but also in obedience to them, keeping their words and deeds in mind, showing them respect and treating them as important, agreeing with what they say, remaining quiet, and putting up with how they treat us unless it violates the first three commandments, and providing them as needed with food, clothing, and shelter. God said on purpose that we should *honor* them, not that we should *love* them, although we should do that as well. Honor is superior to simple love and includes a certain fear that is joined with love and makes people more afraid to insult their parents than punishment would do—just as we honor a holy place with a certain fear but do not flee from it as we would from punishment but flock to it. That kind of fear mixed with love is true honor. Fear without love, however, opposes the things that we despise or flee, as a person fears punishment or the executioner. No honor is present there, only fear without love; indeed, it is fear with hatred and hostility. There is an adage in St. Jerome: "What we fear we also hate."[v] God will not be feared or honored with such fear, nor

---

v   Jerome, Letter 82 to Theophilus (d. 412), bishop of Alexandria, par. 3: "There is an old saying: whomever one fears, one hates; whomever one hates, one wishes to see dead" (MPL 22, col. 737). The saying, which Luther cites elsewhere (WA 13:435), is attributed to the Roman poet Quintus Ennius (239–169 BCE).

does he want parents to be honored that way but honored instead with fear that is combined with love and trust.ᵂ

2. This work may seem easy, but few people take it seriously enough. If the parents are upright and do not love their children according to the fleshˣ but, as they should, direct them and point them toward serving God in word and deed according to the first three commandments, then the selfish will of their children is broken continuously so that they must constantly do, avoid, or suffer exactly what their own nature would rather not do. As a result, the children have reason to despise their parents, murmur against them, or do worse things. Love and fear cannot survive in a child as long as God's grace is not present. Similarly, when parents exercise discipline and punishment as they should—even unjustly at times, although it does no harm to the soul's salvation—one's corrupt nature receives it grudgingly. Above all this, some children are so wicked that they are ashamed of their parents if they are poor, lowborn, unsightly, or dishonorable. Such things matter more to those children than the exalted commandment of God, who is over everything else and gives them such parents out of thoughtful care in order to exercise and train them in his command. It becomes worse when the children have their own children, for whom their love grows, while the love and respect toward their own parents decreases greatly.

What is commanded and said in respect to parents also applies to those who stand in their stead when the parents are not present or have died: friends, stepparents, godparents, civil lords, and spiritual fathers. Everyone must be ruled and be subject to others.[99] Hence we see how many good works are taught in this commandment, since it subjects our entire lives to other people. And from this arises this high praise of obedience and the fact that it comprises all kinds of virtue and good works.

99. In Luther's political and religious world, this was the case. Only close friends were considered equals.

w   Luther would continue to make this connection throughout his career. See the *Small Catechism*, "Ten Commandments," 1–2 (BC, 351), and the *Large Catechism*, "Ten Commandments," 322–25 (BC, 429–30).

x   That is, "do not spoil them."

3. There is a second way of dishonoring parents that is more subtle and dangerous than the first and yet is dressed up and made presentable as genuine honor. It happens whenever natural love causes parents to let children have their own way. Honor and love are present, to be sure, and everyone is delighted; father and mother are pleased, and so are the children.

The plague is so common that examples of the first kind of dishonor (that is, disobedience) are scarcely ever seen. It all happens because parents are so blind that they neither acknowledge nor honor God in the first three commandments and therefore cannot see what their children lack and how they as parents should teach and rear them. As a result, children are taught to value worldly honor, desires, and material goods in order to please other people and go far in life. The children, of course, are quite content and happy to be obedient without any disagreement whatsoever.

Under this seemingly good appearance, however, God's commandment crashes to earth, and what is written in Isaiah and Jeremiah about children being devoured by their own parents is being fulfilled.ʸ The parents are acting just like King Manasseh, who let his own child be sacrificed to the idol Moloch and immolated.ᶻ How is offering one's own child to an idol and immolating it different from parents rearing their children to care for the world more than for God? Such parents simply let their children wander off and be burned up by worldly lust and affections, earthly pleasures, goods, and honor, while love for God, divine honor, and the desire for eternal goods are extinguished.

O how dangerous it is to be a father or mother when only flesh and blood rule! For truly this commandment determines whether or not the first three and the last six are accepted and obeyed, because parents are commanded to teach their children such things, as in Ps. 78[:5-6]. It states: "He commanded our parents to teach . . . their children that the next generation might know them and the child of their

y   Isa. 57:5; Jer. 7:31; 32:35.
z   2 Kgs. 21:6; 23:10.

child might proclaim them to their children."[a] This is the reason that God commands that parents be honored, that is, be loved with fear; for the love just described lacks fear and is consequently more like disrespect than honor.

Now see if it is not true that everyone has enough good works to do, whether a parent or a child! But we who are blind overlook these things and search elsewhere for all kinds of works that are not commanded.

4. When parents are so foolish as to rear their children in a worldly manner, their children should not obey them at all, for according to the first three commandments, God should be more highly esteemed than parents.[100] By the term "rearing in a worldly manner," I mean that children are taught to seek only the pleasure, honor, property, or power of this world.

Of course, it is a necessity and no sin at all to dress appropriately and to earn one's bread honestly. Nevertheless, in their hearts children must be or learn to be reconciled to the fact that it is a pity that this bleak earthly life may hardly begin or be lived without more fancy clothing and possessions than needed for covering the body, warding off the cold, and obtaining enough to eat. Thus, children, while preferring not to do what the world wants and for the sake of something better, must put up with such foolishness and profligacy in order to avoid something even worse. For this reason Queen Esther wore her royal crown and nevertheless said to God: "You know that the symbol of royalty on my head has never pleased me; I consider it no better than filthy rags and never wear it when I am alone but only in public when I must."[b] Whoever thinks like this in their heart wears finery without danger, for they wear it as if not wearing it, dance as if not dancing, live well as if not living well. These

100. This argument about natural parents Luther will then apply to obedience to the church, reflecting his own case with Rome.

a   A close paraphrase of the Vulgate.

b   These words occur in the prayer of Esther that appears only in an expanded Greek version of the book as part of the Apocrypha. These Greek additions were translated into Latin and placed at the end of Esther in the Vulgate and in the 1530s translated into German and for the Wittenberg Bible. In the NRSV, the words quoted by Luther appear in the English translation of the Greek version of Esther and contained in addition C of "Esther with Additions," 14:16.

are secret souls, the hidden brides of Christ, but they are rare because it is hard not to desire fine clothes and jewels. At the command of her parents, St. Cecilia wore robes embroidered with gold, but underneath against her body she wore a hair shirt.[101]

Some parents ask: "How am I supposed to introduce my child to society and ensure for them an honorable marriage? I have to display some finery." Tell me, are these not the words of a heart that doubts God and trusts its own caring about such things more than God's, even though St. Peter teaches [1 Pet. 5:7]: "Cast all your care upon him and be certain that he cares for you"? It is a sign that these parents have never thanked God for their children, never prayed for them in the right way, and never commended them to God. Otherwise they would have learned and experienced how they should expectantly pray to God regarding their children's marriage. Therefore, God lets them follow their own course filled with cares and worries and yet without any chance of success.

5. Thus, it is true, as they say, that parents, if they had done nothing else, can gain salvation by means of their children. And if parents raise them for serving God, then they really have both hands full of good works for themselves. For who are the hungry, thirsty, naked, imprisoned, sick, and strangers[c] save the souls of your own children? With them God makes your house into a hospice with you as the administrator. You are to watch over them, by giving them "food and drink" with good words and works so that they learn to trust, believe, fear, and put their hope in God; honor God's name; refrain from swearing and cursing; and discipline themselves with prayer, fasting, keeping vigils, working, worshiping, hearing God's word, and observing the Sabbath.[102] In this way they will learn to disdain temporal things, endure misfortune with equanimity, face death without fear, not holding this life too dear.

Do you see what an important lesson it is and how many good works are right there for you in your own house with your child, who needs all kinds of things as a hungry, thirsty,

101. According to tradition, Cecilia was an early Christian martyr who was made a saint in the Roman Church. The detail mentioned by Luther appears in the account of her life in the *Golden Legend*, a popular collection of saints' lives compiled in the thirteenth century by Jacobus de Voragine (c. 1230–1298). Strictures against such finery were a standard part of late medieval preaching, on which Luther based his comments here. See his work from 1516 on the Ten Commandments, WA 1:452, 15–453, 10.

102. Here Luther summarizes his comments about the works of the first three commandments.

c Matt. 25:31-46.

naked, poor, imprisoned, and sick soul? Oh what a blessed marriage and household that would be where such parents resided; yes, it would be a true church, an elect cloister, even a paradise. About this Ps. 128[:1-4] states: "Blessed are those who fear God and walk in his commandments. You will be nourished with the labor of your hands; therefore, you will be blessed and it will go well with you. Your wife will be like a fruitful vine in your house, and your children will be like young shoots of the olive tree around your table. Behold, therefore, how blessed are those who fear the Lord!" Where are such parents? Where are those who ask about good works? No one wants to come forward. Why? The devil, flesh, and blood draw away from what God has commanded. It does not glitter and therefore counts for nothing. One person runs off to St. James;[d] another makes vows to Our Lady. No one vows to honor God by governing and teaching themselves and their children well. Those whom God has commanded to guard their children in body and soul abandon them and instead want to serve God somewhere else that has not been commanded. There is no bishop who forbids such perverse behavior or preacher who condemns it. In fact, for the sake of avarice these leaders approve such behavior and daily invent more pilgrimages, canonize more saints, and sell more indulgences![103] May God have pity on such blindness!

6. At the same time, there is no easier way for parents to earn hell than with their own children in their own house when they neglect their children and fail to teach them the things listed above. What good would it do parents if they fasted themselves to death, prayed, made pilgrimages, and did all kinds of good works? Neither at their death nor at the last day will God ask about these things but rather demand that they account for their children whom God entrusted to them—as demonstrated by the words of Christ in Luke 23[:28-29]: "You daughters of Jerusalem, do not cry over me but over yourselves and your children. The days will come when you will say: 'Blessed be the wombs that have never

103. Pilgrim sites were always associated with particular saints and had specific amounts of indulgence connected to them.

d See p. 272, n. 24.

given birth and the breasts that have never suckled.'" Why will they lament in this way if not because their damnation stems from their own children; if the parents had not had them, they might have been saved! To be sure, these words should really open the eyes of parents so they can look spiritually at the souls of their children, lest these poor children be deceived by their parents' false, fleshly love into thinking they had properly honored their parents by not being cross with them or by obeying them in worldly ostentation. Then the children's self-will becomes stronger, although this commandment would have parents be honored when the self-will of their children is broken and they become humble and gentle.

What was said about the other commandments—that they should arise out of the most important work of all[e]—applies here also. No parents should imagine that their discipline or teaching by itself suffices for their children, unless it be done in reliance on God's favor, without any doubt that God is pleased with such works. And let such works be nothing other than for encouraging and practicing one's faith: to trust God and to expect from his merciful will all that is good. Without such faith, no work is efficacious, good, or pleasing; for many unbelievers have reared their children beautifully, but all to no avail because of unbelief.

7. **The second work** of this commandment is to honor and obey our spiritual mother, the holy Christian church, and its spiritual authorities. We should follow whatever they command, forbid, set down, order, ban, or allow. Just as we honor, fear, and love our natural parents, so also we should let the spiritual authorities be right in all matters that do not contradict the first three commandments.[104]

This second work is almost more difficult than the first. The spiritual authorities are supposed to punish sin with the ban and other legal measures and to urge their spiritual children to be upright, so they might have cause to perform these works and exercise themselves by obeying and honoring the authorities. One sees no such diligence now, however,

104. Luther would continue throughout his life to urge obedience to pastors and other spiritual authorities, but always with this caveat, which was where he thought the papacy fell short.

e   That is, from faith.

and they set themselves against their subjects like the mothers who run away from their children to their lovers, as Hos. 2[:7] states.^f They do not preach, teach, guard against anything, or punish anybody. There is no longer any spiritual authority in Christendom.

What then can I say about this second work? There still remain some fast days and festivals that ought to be abolished. But no one pays any attention to this. Excommunication is customarily used only against people in debt, but it should not be that way. The job of the spiritual authorities is to punish severely public sins and scandalous behavior such as adultery, unchastity, usury, gluttony, worldly ostentation, fancy dress, and the like and to see to it that behavior improves. Moreover, they should provide due oversight of clerical chapters, cloisters, parishes, and schools and to ascertain that worship services are properly held. In the schools and cloisters, they should provide learned, upright men^g for the youth, boys and girls, so that all of them are properly educated, their elders provide good examples, and Christendom is filled and adorned with fine young folk. St. Paul writes to his disciple Titus [2:1-10] that he should instruct and be guide to every station in life—young and old, men and women. Now, however, all^h who want to may apply, and those who have only themselves for supervisors and teachers get the job. Alas, it has come to the point that the places in which one should learn the right things have become nothing but schools for rogues and no one cares about the wild young people at all.

8. If this order were followed, then one could say how honor and obedience should take place. But now what is happening is the same as with natural parents who let children have their own way. The spiritual authorities impose a penalty, but then they offer a dispensation, take money for

---

f   By using the German word *Bullen* for "lovers," Luther may be alluding to papal bulls.

g   *Männer* (*Menner* in Luther's text), that is, male teachers. Later, Luther would encourage hiring female teachers for the girls. See *To the Councilmen of Germany* (1524), LW 45:368-71.

h   Singular in the original.

it, and let people get by with more than they should.[105] I will say nothing further. We see that there is more of this than there should be. Greed sits on the throne, and the authorities actually teach what they should prevent. Anyone can see that the spiritual estate[i] is worldlier in all matters than the worldly estate itself. Because of this, Christendom will perish and this commandment will cease to exist.

If there existed a bishop who would diligently provide care and oversight for all such walks of life,[j] make official visits to all the parishes, and stay on top of things, as he ought, then one city alone would truly be too much for him. At the time of the apostles, when Christendom was at its best, every city had its own bishop, even though Christians were a minority in those cities. How could that possibly work today when one bishop has so much to care for, another perhaps more, yet another who claims the whole world, and another half the world?[106] Now is the time to ask God for mercy. We have too many "spiritual authorities" but little or no spiritual governance. Meanwhile, let those who can see to it that clerical chapters, cloisters, parishes, and schools are properly organized and supervised. It would also be the job of spiritual authorities to reduce the number of cloisters and schools if they cannot be provided for. It is much better to have no cloister or clerical chapter than one with bad governance, which would make God angrier.

9. Because these authorities have totally neglected and twisted their proper duties, it must surely follow that they will abuse their power and undertake improper and corrupt works, like parents who command something that is against God. Hence we must be wise, for the Apostle [Paul] has said it will be a dangerous time when such authorities govern,[k] because it will look as if one is challenging their authority if one fails to carry out or defend every order issued by them. We must take the first three commandments and the right

105. A reference to the widespread practice of allowing dispensations from canon law. For example, illegitimate sons could purchase legitimacy so that they could become priests; Archbishop Albrecht von Brandenburg of Mainz (1490–1545) purchased a dispensation to hold more than one episcopal see; in the form of indulgences, priests could purchase the right to celebrate Mass in a territory under the ban.

106. That is, not only are the dioceses too large to provide the pastoral care and supervision they should, but also papal claims to rule the entire church (and world) are also at fault.

---

i   See p. 301, note v.

j   Here and throughout these paragraphs the German is *Stand* or (plural) *Stände*, see above, p. 310, n. 78.

k   See 1 Tim. 4:1-3 and 2 Tim. 3:1-5.

107. Especially notorious was the awarding of bishoprics to members of prominent families on the basis of the candidate's ability and willingness to pay in return. The buying and selling of church offices, known as simony (after Simon Magus in Acts 8:18-24), was strongly condemned in the Middle Ages. Foundations established benefices, that is, guaranteed income attached to clerical duties at a particular place. Holders of such benefices sometimes never even visited them but simply paid an underling (curate) to do the pastoral work involved. Luther also makes similar complaints in the *Address to the Christian Nobility*. See below, p. 405f.

tablet*ᴵ* in our hands and be certain of this: that no person—neither bishop, pope, nor angel—has the right to command or dictate anything that contradicts, hinders, or fails to promote those three commandments with their works. If they do try it, it is invalid and will not stand up, and we commit sin if we obey or follow such things or just stand by and allow it.

It is easy to understand why the rules about fasting do not apply to sick people, pregnant women, or to any and all*ᵐ* who cannot fast without injury to themselves. But let us go further. In our day, nothing comes out of Rome but a yearly fair of spiritual goods that are publicly and shamelessly bought and sold: indulgences, parishes, cloisters, bishoprics, and cathedral chapters—along with all kinds of foundations far and wide set up for the service of God.[107] In this way, not only is all the world's money and property pushed and pulled toward Rome—something that does only minor damage—but parishes, bishoprics, and other prelatures are disrupted, abandoned, and desolate. As a result, the people are completely neglected, God's word, name, and honor are vanishing, and faith is obliterated. In the end, those clerical offices and institutions will belong not only to unlearned and unskilled clerics but also to the biggest Roman buffoons in the world. Thus, everything instituted for God's service—preaching to, guiding, and improving the people—must now be done by stable boys and mule drivers or, lest I put it even more crudely, by Roman whores and buffoons. But still, the only thanks we receive is that they ridicule our people as fools.

10. Seeing that such unbearable shenanigans take place in the name of God and St. Peter, as if God's name and spiritual authority were instituted in order to blaspheme God's honor and to destroy the whole Christian church in body and soul, it is our duty to resist it as much as we can, like upright children whose parents have gone mad. We must first examine the origin of the right that whatever has been

l   For the two tablets of the law, see p. 303, n. 66.
m   Singular in the original.

established in our lands for the service of God and the welfare of our children should benefit Rome, while here, where it should be a benefit, it is neglected. How can we be so dumb?

Since our bishops and spiritual prelates stand stock-still and neither defend themselves or are frightened [about the abuses] and cause Christendom to go to ruin, we should first humbly ask God to help us ward off these things and then get to work putting up roadblocks for these papal courtiers and envoys[108] and, in a mild and reasonable manner, solemnly ask them whether or not they intend to care properly for their benefices, live on-site, and improve the people by means of preaching and setting a good example. If not, and they continue to live in Rome or elsewhere and let their churches become weak and desolate, let the pope in Rome, whom they serve, feed them.[109] It is not right for us to support the pope's servants and his people, that is, his buffoons and whores, to the ruin and injury of our souls.

Do you see? They are the real Turks*n* whom the kings, princes, and nobility should attack first, not for themselves but only for the betterment of Christendom and to prevent blasphemy and the shame done to God's name. Thus, princes should treat these spiritual authorities as they would a father who has lost his wits, where, if one failed to take him into custody and restrain him (albeit with deference and respect), he would ruin his children, his legacy, and everyone else. In like manner, we should hold the Roman authorities in honor as our supreme father but, seeing that they have become so mad and foolish, not allow their schemes so that they cannot use them to destroy Christendom.

11. Some people think we should present this issue to a general council, but I say no to this because we have held many councils where this was proposed, namely, at Constance, Basel, and the last at Rome.[110, 111] Nothing was accomplished, and things got even worse. Such councils are useless because the shrewd minds at Rome devised a ploy that the kings and princes must swear to let them remain as they

108. Messengers who delivered indulgence letters and papal edicts from Rome to other places. Luther may be thinking of the likes of the legate Karl von Miltitz (c. 1490–1529), who had most recently been negotiating with the electoral Saxon court about this case.

109. At this time, some of Germany bishops and other church leaders were, in fact, absentee Italians living in Rome. This was a typical complaint raised in *gravamina* brought to the diets of the Holy Roman Empire. See also the *Address to the Christian Nobility*, below, p. 402.

110. Three late medieval councils whose agendas included church reform: Constance (1414–1418), Basel (1431–1439), and the Fifth Lateran, at Rome (1512–1517).

111. In his struggles with Rome, Luther twice appealed to a general council above the papal decisions, and this continued to comprise a part of the Evangelicals' negotiating position at least through 1530 and the Diet of Augsburg.

n See p. 319 above.

112. As throughout his life and based upon late medieval usage, Luther employs the term *reformacion* to mean not "the Reformation" but substantial or lasting reform of ecclesial institutions.

are with what they possess. Thus, they slammed the door to fend off any kind of reformation[112] and gave free rein and sanction to every kind of villainous behavior, despite the fact that such an oath is required, demanded, and taken against God and the rule of law—and it even excludes the Holy Spirit, who should govern councils. The best and indeed the only remaining remedy would be for kings, princes, the nobility, cities, and communities to take the first step in the matter so that the bishops and clergy, who are now fearful, would have cause to follow. For here one should and must look no further than to God's first three commandments, against which neither Rome, nor heaven, nor earth can command or forbid anything. Imposing the ban and using threats, by which they try to resist such things, makes no difference, just as it makes no difference for a crazed father to threaten a son harshly who resists or challenges him.

12. **The third work** of this commandment is to obey civil authorities, as Paul teaches in Rom. 13[:1-7] and Titus 3[:1] and as St. Peter teaches in 1 Pet. 2[:13-17]. Be subject to the king as the supreme ruler and to the princes as his delegates and to all the ranks of worldly power. Its work is to protect those subject to it and to punish thievery, robbery, and adultery, as St. Paul writes in Rom. 13[:4]: "It does not bear the sword in vain; it serves God by instilling fear in those who are evil [and promoting] the well-being of the godly."

You can sin against civil authorities in two ways. First, when one lies to, deceives, or proves disloyal to them, or fails to carry out with body or property what they have ordered or commanded. Even if the civil authorities commit an injustice, as did the king of Babylon against the people of Israel,*o* God will have them obeyed without any subterfuge or threats. Second, [you sin against civil authorities] when one speaks evil of the authorities, curses them, or, because it is impossible to take revenge, disparages them publicly or in secret with murmuring and destructive criticism.

In all of this, we should bear in mind what St. Peter commanded us to remember: whether the authorities exercise

---

o   Jer. 27:8-15; Bar. 2:19-26.

their power justly or unjustly, it cannot hurt the soul but only the body and what we possess.[p] Even if it happened that they wanted to force us publicly to commit injustice against God or other people, as rulers did in ages past when they were not yet Christian or, as some report, the Turk still does, to suffer injustice destroys no one's souls but instead improves them, even though it may well diminish one's body and property. To commit injustice, however, destroys the soul even if it benefits the entire world.[q]

13. This is why, when injustice is done, civil authorities pose less danger than spiritual ones. Civil authority cannot do harm because it has nothing to do with preaching, faith, and the first three commandments.[113] But spiritual authority does harm not only when it commits injustice but also when it abandons its office and does something different, even if it were better than the best possible action by civil authority. Hence one must resist spiritual authorities when they act unjustly but must not resist civil authorities even though they act equally unjustly. The poor commoners believe and do what they see and hear from the spiritual authorities, and if they do not see and hear it, they will not believe or do anything, because spiritual authority has been established for no reason other than to lead the people in faith to God. All this is not the job of civil authority. For it may do and leave undone whatever it wants, and my faith in God is completely independent and acts on its own, because I do not have to believe whatever civil authority believes. In God's eyes, civil authority is a small matter and is regarded by him as far too insignificant for a person—solely because of it (whether it acts justly or unjustly)—to oppose, disobey, or quarrel with it. On the contrary, spiritual authority is a great, overflowing good and is regarded by God as much too

113. In the 1530s, Luther would modify his opinion and insist that the Christian prince has responsibility to see to it that blasphemy is avoided in his lands.

p   Luther appears to conflate Matt. 10:28 and 1 Pet. 2:18-20.
q   Luther has in mind the common Latin proverb cited in the works of Cicero (*Tusculanae disputationes* 5, 19, 56 [106–43 BCE]): "It is better to suffer injustice than to commit it." See MLStA 2:71, n. 614. Luther's *Table Talk* contains the proverb in the following form: "It is better for us to bear than to do injury, for we sin when we do it but not when we bear it" (WA TR 4:308, no. 4427).

precious, for even the humblest Christian to suffer in silence when it deviates from its own office by even a hair's breadth, not to mention when it completely violates its office as we observe every day.

14. There are also various abuses connected to civil authority, first, by succumbing to flatterers, which is a common and particularly damaging scourge to this authority. No one can guard against or watch out for this enough. It is led around by the nose, rides roughshod over the poor commoners, and becomes a government, as the sage said, like a spider's web that catches small flies but lets the millstones pass right through.[114] The laws, orders, and governance of civil authority catch the small fry but let the big fish escape. If the lord is not bright enough to do without his advisers' counsel or is not so well regarded that they fear him, then their authority must needs be childish, unless God somehow performs a miracle.

For this reason, God has deemed evil and incompetent rulers the worst plague of all and added this threat in Isa. 3[:1]: "I will take all brave men from you and give you children and childish rulers." In the Scriptures (Ezek. 14[:12-23]), God has identified four plagues. The first and least of these, which David also chose, is pestilence;[r] the second is uncontrolled inflation; the third is war; the fourth, all kinds of wild beasts—lions, wolves, serpents, and dragons. These beasts stand for evil rulers because, wherever they are, not only does the land suffer ruin in body and possessions, as in the first two plagues, but it also suffers the loss of honor, discipline, virtue, and the salvation of souls. For pestilence and inflation make people upright and rich, but war and wicked rulers destroy everything that makes for earthly and eternal well-being.

15. It takes a really intelligent lord not always to force the issue even though he may have justice and the best possible case on his side. It is a much nobler virtue to put up with injury to one's rights than to property and the body, since

114. A common European proverb, found also in Spanish and Russian, and often used by Luther. See Wander, 4:723.

r   2 Sam. 24:10-17.

the subjects benefit from such restraint, especially given that earthly justice only depends on temporal goods.

Thus, this is a foolish saying: "I have a right to that, and I will take it by force and keep it although it brings nothing but misfortune to another."[115] We read that the emperor Octavian[116] would not go to war no matter how just the cause, unless there was some indication it would do more good than harm or that the harm would not be unbearable. He said: "War is like fishing with a golden net; one never catches enough to make up for the risk of losing much more."[s] Someone leading a wagon must travel quite differently than when he is simply walking alone. The latter can walk, jump, and do as he pleases, but when leading, he must steer and conduct himself in such a way that the horse and wagon can follow, and he must pay more attention to them than to his own wishes. The same is true of a lord, who leads the public with him. He must not travel or act as he pleases but in accord with the public's abilities, and he must consider what is necessary and most useful to them more than his own will and desires. For when a lord rules only according to his crazy ideas and only follows his own discretion, he is like a crazy driver who hurtles their horses and wagons wildly over unfamiliar roads and bridges through thickets, hedges, ditches, rushing streams, hills, and valleys. He won't drive very far before it ends in a complete wreck.

For this reason, it would be best for rulers if, starting in their youth, they would read or have read to them histories from both sacred and pagan books, in which they would discover more examples about the art of ruling than all the law books. One can read in Esther 6[:1-2] that the kings of Persia did this. Examples and histories always offer and teach more than laws and jurisprudence. The former teaches on the basis of sure and certain experience, while the latter teaches using uncertain, untried words.

115. A saying similar to the Latin: *Fiat iustitia et pereat mundus* ("Let justice be done, and let the world perish"), also attributed Pope Adrian VI (1459–1523), who became pope in the 1522. See MLStA 2:73, n. 629.

116. Gaius Octavius (63 BCE–CE 14), that is, Caesar Augustus, the first Roman emperor.

Octavian Augustus.
Bust kept since 1589
in Palace Bevilacqua, Verona.

s   For this common proverb, see MLStA 2:73, n. 633. The Roman historian Flavius Eutropius (4th cent.), *Breviarium ab urbe condita* VII.14, used this phrase to describe and criticize Caesar Augustus's successor, Nero (37-68). For Caesar Augustus's reluctance to go to war, see Suetonius (69– d. after 122), *Divus Augustus*, 21, 2.

117. By "this land" Luther is thinking of the German lands of the Holy Roman Empire. For a broader discussion of the topic in sections 16 and 17, see *Address to the Christian Nobility*, pp. 460–64, below.

118. German: *Zinskauf*. It was the practice of paying a sum of money from the buyer to the seller, which then made the seller responsible for paying the buyer a fixed percentage of the purchase price each year in perpetuity. Originally, it involved land and thus was a purchase of the land's income. These contracts were first constructed to circumvent the church's strictures on charging interest. See Luther's extensive criticism in *Trade and Usury* (final version: 1524) in LW 45:295–310, a section first published in a 1520 sermon attacking the practice.

119. Luther refers to a German saying that the "three Jews" (a term of obvious derision) are "shorn Jews" (i.e., priests), "Jews carrying golden rings" (Christian merchants who charge more interest than Jewish bankers), and "circumcised Jews" (the actual Jewish people). Because Christians were not supposed to charge interest to fellow Christians, the task of loaning money often fell to Jewish people, which became yet one more basis for anti-Jewish propaganda. See Wander, 2:1034f.

120. German: *Officiel*. This was the title of a specific episcopal officer, who carried out the bishop's will.

16. In our day, all rulers, especially in this land, have three especially necessary works to perform.[117] First, they should do away with the dreadful habits of gluttony and drunkenness, not only because of the excess but also because of the expense. Owing to the spice trade and the like, without which one could live quite well, there has been no small decline in temporal goods in this land, and it continues each day. The secular government would have enough on its hands to prevent both these rampant vices that have pervaded the land far and wide, and it could perform no better service for God, and it would improve its own land. Second, they should restrict the outlandish cost of clothing, on which so much wealth is wasted and which merely serves the world and the flesh. It is appalling that this abuse is so prevalent among a people that is pledged, baptized, and dedicated to the crucified Christ and should carry the cross with him and should daily prepare themselves for that other life through dying. If this practice were only observed in a few cases due to imprudence, it would be more bearable; but since it is done freely, with impunity, and without hindrance or shame, and since both praise and fame are sought for doing it, such waste is truly an un-Christian enterprise. Third, the rulers should abolish the usurious practice of purchasing income,[118] which ruins, devours, and destroys all kinds of lands, cities, and people all over the world through its devious appearance of not really being usury at all, when in fact it is worse than usury because one does not take precautions as one does when usury is obvious. See, this is the three Jews (as it is said) who suck out the entire world.[119] On this point, the lords should not sleep or be lazy if they want to give God a good account of their office.

17. The chicanery perpetrated by church officials[120] and other episcopal and clerical officers should be pointed out here. For the sake of making a penny, they place tremendous burdens on the poor commoners through excommunications, subpoenas, harassment, and coercion. Such actions should be prohibited by secular authority*t* because no other assistance or means of stopping this are available.

O would God in heaven that once such a government, as the people of Israel had, would also start to abolish houses of prostitution!*u* It is an un-Christian image and a public sin for Christians to maintain such houses that in earlier times were completely unheard of. A new law should require that boys and girls be married in a timely fashion in order to avoid this vice. Both spiritual and civil authorities should support such an ordinance and practice. If it was possible for the Jews, why should it not also be possible for Christians? Indeed, if such a law is possible in villages, market towns, and a few cities, as is evident, why is it not possible everywhere?

What prevents this is that there is no government in the world. No one wants to work, and so the artisans have to lay their journeymen off. Then they run wild and no one can tame them. If there were an ordinance that they would have to obey their masters and that no one would hire them elsewhere, this loophole for evil would be closed. God help me, I worry that desiring such a law is only wishful thinking, but we are not thereby excused.

Please notice that I have identified only a few works of those in authority, but nevertheless they are so beneficial and so many that they have a surfeit of good works with which they can serve God every minute. Like all the others, these works should arise from faith and exercise faith, so that no one does them to curry favor with God but rather, certain of his graciousness, does them to the honor and praise of their dear and merciful God and to serve and be useful to one's neighbors.

18. **The fourth work** of this commandment is for household servants to obey the man and woman of the house and for workers to obey their masters and mistresses. On this matter, St. Paul says in Titus 2: "Preach ... to laborers or servants*v* that they are to hold their masters in honor, obey

---

t   Literally, "the worldly sword," the common designation for temporal government.

u   See Lev. 19:29; Deut. 23:17-18.

v   German: *den knechten odder dienern*: Luther's standard paraphrase for the Latin *servi* ("servants" or "slaves").

them, do what pleases them, and neither deceive nor resist them. By so doing, they also do credit to the teaching of Christ and to our faith, so that nonbelievers will have no reason to complain about or resent us."[w] Saint Peter says [1 Pet. 2:18-19]: "Servants, obey your masters out of fear of God, not only those who are kind and gentle but also those who are capricious and rough, for it is pleasing to God when a person innocently bears injustice."

One of the biggest complaints in the world is about servants and workers, how they are disobedient, disloyal, crude, and greedy, in short, a plague from God.[121] Truth be told, obedience is the only job of servants by which they can be saved; they really do not need to take off on pilgrimages or do anything else of the kind. They have enough to do if their hearts are set in the right direction, gladly doing or avoiding what they know will please their masters and mistresses and doing it all in simple faith, not that they thereby would merit a lot but that they do everything relying on God's grace, where all merit is located,[x] working without reward, purely out of love and goodwill toward God that has grown out of this trust. Moreover, they should allow all such work to be a kind of exercise and admonition that will increase their faith and trust more and more. As we have said now many times, this faith makes all works good. Indeed, faith itself must do them and be the "master artisan."[y]

19. At the same time, masters and mistresses should not rule their servants, maids, and workers with an iron hand or be too exacting. Instead, now and then they should ease up and overlook some things to keep peace.[z] For the same criteria may not fit equally at all times for all situations of life, because here on earth we lead imperfect lives. Saint Paul says in Col. 4[:1]: "Masters, treat your slaves justly and fairly and remember that you also have a master in heaven." Just as

121. In Luther's day, servants (German: *Knechte*) were usually young people indentured for a time to a household to learn agriculture or a trade. They received wages, room and board, and they could become householders or artisans in their own right. Day laborers (German: *Tagelöhner*) were paid daily wages by farmers or other householders. Lifelong slavery and serfdom were unknown in Luther's day in Saxony.

---

w   A conflation of Titus 2:1a, 9-10 with 1 Tim. 6:1-2.

x   The word for "merit" in German also means "earn."

y   German: *Werkmeister.* See above, p. 281, note o.

z   Literally, "look through the fingers," a favorite phrase of Luther also for how God overlooks sin.

masters do not wish to be treated harshly by God but rather want many things to be overlooked through grace, so also they should treat their servants all the more gently and overlook some things, while at the same time making sure that their servants do right and learn to fear God.

Look at the good works a mistress and master can do and look at the fine way in which God constantly makes good works available to us in such variety and so directly that we have no need to inquire about them and can now ignore the other showy and popular works that people have dreamed up, for example, pilgrimages, building churches, acquiring indulgences, and the like. Here I should also mention that a wife should be subject to her husband as her superior, obey and yield to him, be silent, and let him be in the right as long as it is not against God. At the same time, a man should love his wife, let some things go, and not be too strict or exacting in dealing with her. Saints Peter and Paul said a great deal about this matter,*a* but it properly belongs to a longer treatment of the commandments and is easily grasped from these passages.

20. Everything we have said about these works is covered by two words: *obedience* and *solicitude*. Obedience is the duty of subjects, and solicitude is the duty of superiors, who should be diligent in ruling their subjects well, dealing with them kindly, and doing everything in their power to be useful and helpful to them. That is their way to heaven and the best work they can do on earth, more pleasing to God than if they would perform nothing but miracles. Therefore, St. Paul says in Rom. 12[:8], "Let the works of those in authority be solicitude." As if he were saying: "These individuals*b* are not led astray by what people with a different rank or walk of life are doing; they do not try to copy this or that work, whether glittering or drab; rather, they attend to their own walk of life and consider how they can be useful to those under their authority. They persist in that and refuse to be torn away even if heaven stood open before them or to

a Eph. 5:22-25; Col. 3:18-19; 1 Pet. 3:5-7.
b Singular in the original.

flee even if hell itself were running after them. That is the right road, which will take them to heaven."

Truly, those people, therefore, who attend only to themselves and their own walk of life and stand by them will quickly become people who are rich in good works, but so quietly and secretly that no one will see it but God. Now, however, we let all this go and instead one person runs to the Carthusians,[122] another here, another there, just as if good works and God's commandments were thrown in a corner and covered up. In Prov. 1[:20-21], on the contrary, it is written: "Wisdom cries out openly in the streets, in the midst of the people, and at the gates of the city." This demonstrates that good works are available in abundance everywhere, all the time, in all walks of life. Christ himself proclaimed it in Matt. 24[:23-26]: "When they tell you that Christ is here or he is there, do not believe them; when they say, 'Look, he is in the wilderness,' do not go out, or 'Look, he is hidden inside the house,' do not believe it. They are false prophets and false Christians."[c]

21. At the same time, obedience is the obligation of subjects, who with all diligence and thoroughness are to do or avoid whatever those over them demand, not allowing themselves to be sidetracked from this, regardless of what others are doing. They should never imagine they would be better off doing other good works—be it prayer or fasting or whatever it is called—that would divert them from carrying out their duties with careful and persistent effort.

Should it ever happen, however, as it often does, that temporal power and authority, whatever their titles, force subjects to act against God's commandment or keeps them from obeying it, then obedience ceases and duty is set aside. In that case, one must say what St. Peter said to the leaders of the Jews: "One must obey God more than mortals."[d] He did not say: "mortals should not be obeyed," for that would

122. A monastic order founded in 1084 in France and known for its strict vows of renunciation and silence.

c   The term "false Christians" appears in the Latin text.
d   Acts 5:29. The Latin text may be rendered either "rather than" or, as Luther does here, "more than."

be false, but "God . . . more than mortals." If a prince, for example, wanted to start a war but it was known that the cause was unjust, then no one should follow him or help him because God has commanded that we should not kill our neighbors or do them an injustice. Likewise if the prince commanded giving false testimony, robbing, lying, deceiving someone, and the like. One should instead let property, honor, and life go so that God's commandment may abide.

On the Fifth Commandment[e]

The first four commandments do their work on human reason. That is, they take human beings captive, rule them, and make them subjects, so that they do not rule themselves, think for themselves, or think too much of themselves but instead show humility and let themselves be led in order to protect against arrogance. The following commandments take up human desires and lusting in order to slay them.[123]

1. There are the angry and vengeful passions of which the fifth commandment speaks: "You shall not kill." The work of this commandment is very comprehensive, drives out vice, and is called gentleness. This gentleness is of two kinds. The first kind sparkles beautifully, but there is nothing behind it. We direct it to friends and to others who help and support us in matters that concern our property and reputation or who do not injure us in word or in deed. Such gentleness can also be expressed by irrational animals, lions and snakes, pagans, Jews, Turks, fools, murderers, and evil women.[124] All of them can be gentle and serene as long as one does what they want or leaves them in peace. Not a few people, deceived by such apparent gentleness, however, then try to justify and excuse their anger by saying: "I would not be angry if everyone left me in peace." Oh, sure, my dear! Under these circumstances the evil spirit would also be gentle if everything went its way. Sorrow and strife overwhelm you because they are meant to show you to yourself—how stuffed full of anger

123. Luther employs a basic philosophical distinction between intellect (reason) and will (desires).

124. Luther expresses typical disdain for outsiders to his community. The term "evil woman" often specifically referred either to prostitutes or witches.

_e_ Exod. 20:13; Deut. 5:17.

and malice you are. In this way, you are admonished to strive toward gentleness and to expel your anger.

The other kind of gentleness is good to the core and is revealed toward adversaries and enemies. It does not hurt them, does not take revenge; does not curse, insult, or spread lies about them; does not even wish bad things on them, even though they might have taken away property, reputation, body, friends—everything. Wherever possible, this gentleness returns good for evil, speaks well of them, wishes them the best, and prays for them. For Christ says in Matt. 5[:44]: "Return good for evil; pray for your persecutors and those who revile you." And Paul says in Rom. 12[:14]: "Bless those who curse you; do not curse them but treat them well."

2. Now see just how this precious and exalted work has disappeared among Christians! Nothing reigns more powerfully over all people but quarreling, war, strife, anger, hate, envy, gossip, cursing, blaspheming, doing injury, taking vengeance, and other expressions of anger in word and deed. Yet we go on celebrating feast days, hearing Mass, saying little prayers, endowing churches and [providing them with] ornaments that God has not commanded. We show off these works splendidly and extravagantly, as though we were the holiest Christians the world had ever seen. Meanwhile, using all these mirrors and facades, we allow God's commandment to perish to the point that no one realizes how near or far he [or she] is from gentleness and the fulfillment of this divine commandment, even though God said that those who keep the commandments will enter into eternal life, not those who do these other works.*f*

There is no one alive on earth to whom God does not give an indicator of their*g* own anger and iniquity, that is, by way of their enemies and adversaries, who harm their property, their honor, their bodies, or their friends. In this way, God tests whether or not anger is still present and whether or not they can be gracious to their enemies, speak well of them, treat them kindly, and intend them no harm. Given this,

f   See Matt. 19:16-17; Mark 10:17-19; Luke 18:18-20.

g   Singular in the original throughout this paragraph.

now let those come forth who ask what they should do in order to perform good works, please God, and be saved. Let them visualize their enemies and place them before the eyes of their hearts in order to bend and accustom themselves to thinking well of their enemies, wishing the best for them, caring and praying for them, and when the opportunity presents itself, speaking well of them and doing good to them. Whoever attempts this and does not have enough to do for an entire lifetime may prove me a liar and declare all this talk to be false. Since, however, God will have it this way and not be remunerated in any other way, what does it profit us to go around with great works that are not commanded and to ignore this command? Therefore, God says in Matt. 5[:22]: "If you are angry with a neighbor, you will be liable to judgment; those who say to their neighbors *racha* (that is, a cruel, angry, horrid form of abuse) are liable to the council; those who call their neighbors fools (that is, all kinds of cursing, swearing, insulting, gossiping) are liable to eternal fire." If angry words and thoughts are condemned so severely, how will the actions of the hands—beating, wounding, killing, injuring, wreaking damage, and the like—be judged?

3. Where a profound gentleness is present, the heart bewails every evil that happens to one's enemy. These are the genuine children and heirs of God, the brothers [and sisters] of Christ, who did the same for all of us on the holy cross. Thus we see that an upright judge sorrowfully pronounces a verdict on those who are guilty and is greatly pained by the death sentence required by law for such people. This deed appears as if it arose from anger and cruelty, but the gentleness is so profoundly good that it persists under the angry deeds; indeed, it wells up from the heart most powerfully just when it has to be angry and serious.

We must beware, however, lest we are gentle against God's honor and commandment. For it is written of Moses [Sir. 45:4] that he was the gentlest man on earth, and yet, after the Jews had worshiped the golden calf and angered God, he had many of them killed to placate God once again.[h] It

---

h Exod. 32:28.

is not fitting, therefore, for the authorities to take it easy and allow sin to rule and for us to remain silent about this. I should not be so concerned about my property, my honor, or injury done to me that I become angry; but we must defend God's honor and commandment and guard against injury and injustice done to our neighbors—those who govern using the sword and others using words and rebukes, yet all filled with sorrow for the one who has earned such punishment.

This precious, fine, and sweet work can be learned easily wherever we do it in faith and exercise our faith in doing it. Just as faith does not doubt God's love in that it has a gracious God, so also it can easily be gracious and kind to our neighbors, no matter how seriously they have transgressed [against us], for we have committed even worse transgressions against God. Yes, it is but a short commandment, but it offers within it a long and great exercise for good works and faith.

The Sixth Commandment

"You shall not commit adultery" [i]

1. A good work is also commanded in this commandment. It includes many things, drives out many vices, and is called purity or chastity. About this much has been written and preached so that almost everyone knows about it, even if they do not take it to heart and practice it as diligently as they do the works that are not commanded. (We are quite ready to do what is not commanded and to leave undone what is commanded!) We observe that the world is full of shameful deeds of unchastity, scandalous sayings, fables, and ditties. Moreover, incentives daily pile up to indulge in gluttony, drunkenness, idleness, and excessive displays of jewelry and finery. Meanwhile, we carry on as if we were Christians when we have attended church, said our little

---

i Exod. 20:14; Deut. 5:18.

prayers, and observed our fasts and feast days as if that were enough.

If, however, no other work than chastity were commanded, we would have our hands full obeying it alone. Unchastity is a very dangerous and rabid vice that infects all our members: the heart through our thoughts; the eyes in our looking; the ears through what we hear; the mouth in what we say; our hands, feet, and entire body through what we do. To keep it in check requires enormous work and effort. In this way, God's commandment teaches us what a formidable thing is involved in honest good works. Indeed, it is impossible out of our own powers even to conceive a good work, to say nothing about beginning to do it or bringing it to completion. According to St. Augustine, the struggle for chastity is for individual Christians[j] the hardest struggle of all simply because they must daily defend themselves against it without ceasing and seldom defeat it.[k] All the saints have bemoaned it and shed tears over it, as St. Paul says in Rom. 7[:18]: "I find within me, that is, in my flesh, nothing good."[125]

2. The work of chastity, should it endure, results in many other good works: fasting and moderation against gluttony and drunkenness; vigils and early rising against laziness and oversleeping; labor and effort against idleness. Gluttony, drinking to excess, oversleeping, laziness, and idleness are weapons of unchastity that can quickly overcome chastity. Over against these, the holy Apostle Paul [Rom. 13:12-13] lists fasting, vigilance, and labor as godly weapons that keep unchastity in check, although, as mentioned above, these very disciplines should go no further than to curb unchastity, not to damage one's health.

The strongest defense of all consists of prayer and the word of God. When evil lust stirs, a person should flee to prayer, beg God for mercy and aid, read and contemplate the gospel, and gaze on the suffering of Christ depicted there.

125. The comments in this section especially reflect Luther's situation as an Augustinian friar. Later comments in his 1521 tract, *The Judgment of Martin Luther on Monastic Vows* (LW 44:243–400], and elsewhere demonstrate how he reexamined his understanding of chastity in the years to come.

---

j   Singular in the original.
k   The statement is found in a sermon, still attributed to Augustine in Luther's day, but now assigned to pseudo-Augustine, *Sermon* 293 (MPL 39:2302).

Psalm 137[:9] says: "Blessed are those who seize the children of Babylon and smash them against a rock."[l] This means: as long as our evil thoughts are in their infancy and just beginning, run to the Lord Christ, who is a rock that will pulverize and destroy them.

Do you see? Each and every person will be completely swamped, find enough to do for oneself and be overwhelmed in him- or herself with countless good works. At present, however, no one uses praying, fasting, alertness, and labor to ward off vice; they are considered ends in themselves, even though they were instituted to accomplish the work of this commandment and to cleanse us more and more each day.

Others have identified more things to avoid: soft beds and clothing; expensive jewelry; and the company, conversation, and eyeing of women or men (as the case may be) along with similar things that promote chastity. In such matters, no one can prescribe a binding rule or a fixed amount. All individuals[m] must judge for themselves which of these things—in what amount and used for how long—promote chastity. Then they must choose and keep at them. If they cannot, for a while they should be given into the care of another, who will hold them to what they have chosen until they are able to control themselves. Long ago, cloisters were established for this reason, namely, to teach young people discipline and purity.

3. More obviously than for any other commandment, a sound and robust faith helps in doing this work. For that reason, Isa. 11[:5] states: "Faith is the girdle of his loins," that is, a guardian of chastity; for those who live expecting all grace to come from God are well pleased by spiritual purity. For this reason, they are able to resist more easily the unchastity of the flesh, and in this faith the Spirit tells them how to avoid evil thoughts and everything else that stands

---

l   Luther uses a not unusual allegorical interpretation of this psalm, one that the authors of the *Confutation of the Augsburg Confession* also used as support for clerical celibacy. See Robert Kolb and James A. Nestingen, eds., *Sources and Contexts of The Book of Concord* (Minneapolis: Fortress Press, 2001), 126.

m Singular in the original.

in the way of chastity. Just as faith in divine love lives continually and effects every good work, so it never omits the Spirit's admonitions about everything that either pleases or displeases God, as St. John says in his letter [1 John 2:27]: "You have no need of anyone to instruct you, for God's anointing," meaning God's Spirit, "teaches you all things."

We should not despair when we cannot rid ourselves quickly of such attacks, and we should not imagine that we will be free of them as long as we live. We should consider them as nothing other than inducements and admonitions to pray, fast, do vigils, labor, and practice other things, in order to suppress the flesh and especially to promote and practice faith in God. The chastity to prize is not the kind that comes easily, but rather the kind that takes to the field to battle unchastity and to drive out all the poison that the flesh and evil spirit have injected. Saint Peter says [1 Pet. 2:11]: "I admonish you to keep away from carnal lust and desire that constantly fight against the soul." And St. Paul in Rom. 6[:12] says: "Do not give in to the passions of the body." These verses and others like them demonstrate that no one lacks sinful lust but should and must resist it every day. Although this brings with it unrest and unpleasantness, to God it is still an acceptable work, and for us that should be our consolation and our sufficiency. Those who think they can control such attacks by giving in to lust only make it burn hotter. Even though it may subside for a while, it returns at another time stronger than before and finds human nature weaker than ever.

The Seventh Commandment

"You shall not steal" [n]

[1.] This commandment, too, includes a work that consists of many good works and opposes many vices. In German, it is called "generosity." This is a work that involves each and

[n]   Exod. 20:15; Deut. 5:19.

every individual being ready to use whis or her possessions to help and serve. It fights against not only theft and robbery but any damage to worldly possessions that one person can inflict on another, for example, through greed, usury, overcharging, cheating, selling inferior goods, or using false weights and measures. Who can recount all the clever new tricks that increase every day in business? Everyone searches for an advantage to the disadvantage of others; they forget the law that says [Matt. 7:12]: "Whatever you wish others to do to you, do also to them." All who keep this rule in mind in their crafts, business, and trade with the neighbor will soon find how they should buy and sell, take and give, lend and give at no charge, make promises and keep them, and the like. When we observe the nature of the world, to what extent avarice prevails everywhere, we not only should have enough to do nourishing ourselves with God and honorable [living], but also we also should become filled with dread and fright at this perilous and miserable life that is so weighed down by, besmeared with, and captive to anxiety about daily sustenance and dishonest searching after it.

2. Not in vain does the wise man say [Sir. 31:8-9]: "Blessed is the rich person who is found blameless, who does not run after gold or put trust in its treasures. Who is that person that we may offer praise, for a miracle has been accomplished in that life?" It is as if the author wanted to say, such people are very rare or do not exist at all. Indeed, there are very few people who notice or admit to such addiction to gold; for avarice has a very attractive and respectable cover, namely, bodily nourishment and other natural necessities. Under that cover, greed acts without limits or bounds. Thus, as Sirach says, those who try to live without being touched by greed must indeed accomplish miraculous signs and wonders in their lives.

Now consider this. Those individuals[o] who want to perform not only good works but also miracles, which God praises and that please him, what else would they need to

o   Singular in the original throughout this paragraph.

investigate? Let them examine themselves and make sure they do not run after gold or set their trust in money, but let the gold run after them and the money wait upon their pleasure. If they avoid setting their heart on it or liking it too much, then they are indeed generous miracle workers and blessed ones, as Job 31[:24] states: "I have never relied on gold nor let money be my comfort and confidence." And Ps. 62[:10]: "If riches increase, do not set your heart on them." Christ teaches the same thing in Matt. 6[:31-32]: "We are not to worry about what we eat or drink or how we will clothe ourselves; for God knows what we need and provides it all."

Some people say: "Okay, rely on God, do not worry, and see whether or not a roast hen flies into your mouth."[126] On the contrary, I am not saying we should not work or look for food, but that we should not worry or be greedy or doubt we will have enough. For in Adam, we have all been sentenced to hard work, as God says [Gen. 3:19]: "In the sweat of your face you shall eat your bread." And Job 5[:7]: "As birds are born to fly, so human beings are born to work."[p] As birds fly around without feeling worried or greedy, so we should work without worry and avarice. If you are anxious and greedy to such an extent that you are waiting for a roast hen to fly into your mouth, then be anxious and greedy to see if you are fulfilling God's commandment and going to be saved.

3. Faith by itself teaches the work of this commandment. For if the heart anticipates God's favor and relies on it, how is it possible for faith to be greedy and full of cares? It must be certain beyond any doubt that God receives us. For this reason faith does not cling to any money at all but instead uses it with joyful generosity for the benefit of others—knowing all along that it will have enough for any needs because the God in whom it trusts will never deceive or forsake it, as Ps. 37[:25] says: "I have been young and now am old, yet I have not seen" a believer who trusts in God, that is, "a righteous person forsaken or such a one's children

126. Luther is referring to what happens in a popular medieval tale about a land where roasted fowl fly directly into one's mouth and fried fish jump from the water to one's feet. See p. 259, n. 5 above.

---

p Luther cites the Vulgate, which has "birds" in place of "sparks" (NRSV).

begging bread."[q] This is why the only sin that the Apostle [Paul] calls idolatry is greed [Col. 3:5], because it is the crudest example of not trusting God and expecting more benefit from wealth than from God. Through trust God is truly honored or dishonored, as I said earlier.[r]

Indeed, in this commandment one can clearly see how all good works must arise from and be done in faith. For everyone can see without a doubt that the cause of avarice is mistrust, while the cause of generosity is faith because the person who trusts God is generous and does not have doubts about not having enough at any time. And vice versa: a person is greedy and anxious because of not trusting God. Just as faith is the master artisan[s] and driving force behind the good work of generosity in this commandment, so it is with all the other commandments. Without such faith, generosity accomplishes nothing but seems rather like a careless waste of money.

4. Here it is also important to realize that this same generosity must be extended to enemies and opponents. For as Christ himself teaches in Luke 6[:32-34]: "What kind of good deed is it if you are generous only to your friends? For wicked people do the same for their friends." Even irrational animals are kind and generous to their own species. A Christian, however, must go further and show generosity to those who have not earned it, to evildoers, enemies, and ungrateful folk, and like the heavenly Father "let the sun rise on the evil and on the good and send rain on the grateful and the ungrateful."[t]

Here it becomes clear how difficult it is to do good works according to God's commandment and how human nature resists, squirms, and stalls because it much prefers its own easier, self-chosen works. Therefore, try approaching your

q   Luther places his interpretive gloss in front of the biblical text ("a righteous person").

r   See Luther's treatment of the second commandment, above, p. 269f.

s   German: *Werkmeister*. See above, p.281, note o.

t   Matt. 5:45.

enemies, who show no gratitude, and do good to them. Then you will see how far you are from obeying this commandment and how you will have to work at practicing this work your whole life long. When your enemies need your aid and you fail to help them even though you could, that is just the same as if you had stolen from them, because you are obligated to help them. Thus St. Ambrose says: "Feed the hungry, for if you do not, then you have slain them insofar as it was in your power."ᵘ Works of mercy belong to this commandment, and Christ will ask you about them at the Last Day.[127] Nevertheless, princes and cities should see to it that vagrants, pilgrims,ᵛ and other nonresident beggars are either banned or allowed residency with proper "restrictions and ordinances,"ʷ so that troublemakers posing as beggars are not permitted to get away with their drifting and villainy, of which there is plenty. I have said more about the works of this commandment in my sermon on usury.[128]

The Eighth Commandment

*"You shall not bear false witness against your neighbor"*ˣ

[1.] This commandment appears trivial at first but is in fact so vast that whoever would keep it correctly must stake everything—body and life, goods and reputation, friends and all possessions—on it. And yet it involves only the work of one small bodily member: the tongue. In German, it is

127. "Works of mercy" is a technical term for the works listed in the parable of the sheep and the goats in Matt. 25:35-36.

128. The "large" tract on usury (1520: WA 6:36-60). In the autumn of 1519 Luther had composed a much shorter essay on usury, which he revised and expanded for publication in early 1520 not long before he began to write the *Treatise on Good Works*. In 1524 the expanded treatise on usury was reissued together with a new essay on business practices and monopolies under the title *Trade and Usury* (LW 45:231-310; WA 15:279-313).

---

u   Cited by Luther from medieval canon law, where it is listed with citations from Ambrose of Milan. According to MLStA 2:85. n. 764, it is found in Anselm of Canterbury (c. 1033-1109), citing Polycarp (69-155), and in many other medieval sources, including Bernard of Clairvaux and Gabriel Biel (c. 1420-1495).

v   Literally, *"Jakobsbrüder"* (or James's brothers), that is, pilgrims allegedly on their way to or from the shrine of St. James at Compostela in northwestern Spain.

w   German: *Masse und Ordnung*, a technical legal phrase of the sixteenth century, often found in city ordinances of the time.

x   Exod. 20:16; Deut. 5:20.

called speaking the truth and refuting lies wherever necessary. Thus, many of the tongue's evil works are forbidden here: both those that happen through speaking and those that occur in silence. Through speaking, for example, when someone has a fraudulent case in a court of law and tries to defend it with falsehoods or to trick one's neighbor with deceit—using anything to make one's own case look better and stronger while passing over in silence and downplaying anything that would help the good case of the neighbor. With such behavior, however, these individuals are not treating the neighbor as they would like the neighbor to treat them.[y] Some people act that way out of selfishness, and others do it to avoid damages or disgrace, but either way they are seeking what they want more than God's commandment. As an excuse, they use the saying, "Vigilanti iura subveniunt," (the law helps those who are vigilant),[z] as if they were not obligated to watch out for their neighbor's case as much as for their own. Thus, they intentionally allow their neighbors' case, which they know is just, to be lost. This outrage is so common that I fear no legal judgment or action can take place without one party or the other sinning against this commandment. Even if they cannot succeed in carrying out their intentions, they still had the unjust desire and intention in wanting the just case of their neighbor to lose and their own fraudulent one to be upheld. This sin is especially prevalent in cases where the other party is a big shot[a] or an enemy, because a person wants to take revenge on an enemy and no one wants to antagonize a big shot. Out come the flattery and the smooth talk or even just silence about the truth. No one will risk falling from grace or favor, being injured, or risking any danger for the sake of the truth, and consequently God's commandment must founder. That is

---

y   See Matt. 7:12. Singular in the original.

z   An adage from jurisprudence, often cited by Luther. See MLStA 2:86, n. 776. A longer form (in both Latin and German) reads: "Law is written for the vigilant not for the sleeping." See Wander, 3:1520, n. 46.

a   German: *grosse Hansen* ("big Johns").

pretty much the way the world runs, and those who would resist it have their hands full with good works fulfilled simply by using the tongue. In addition, how many people let themselves be silenced from telling the truth by gifts and bribes, so that in every respect it is truly a noble, great, and rare work for a person not to bear false witness against one's neighbor.

2. Beyond that, however, is a still greater witness of the truth in which we must fight against the evil spirits.[129] And it arises not because of worldly goods but for the sake of the gospel and the truth of the faith, which the evil spirit has never been able to tolerate, and therefore it unceasingly induces the most powerful among the people to oppose the gospel and to persecute it to the point that one can scarcely withstand them. About this Ps. 82[:3-4] states: "Rescue the needy from the power of the unjust and help the forsaken maintain the justice of their cause." The spiritual prelates[130] are at fault for the fact that such persecution has now become rare. They have not emphasized the gospel but have allowed it to be forgotten. In this way, they buried the very thing that caused the persecution and made this witness necessary. In place of the gospel, they teach their own laws and whatever else pleases them. The devil can now remain quiet because, by triumphing over the gospel, he has also crushed faith in Christ so that everything is going according to his plan. If, however, the gospel is emphasized and heard once again, the whole world will assuredly rouse itself and rebel—the majority of the kings, princes, bishops, teachers, clergy, and everything high and mighty will oppose it and become enraged. This has always happened when the word of God comes to light because the world cannot tolerate what comes from God. This is proven in Christ, who was and is the noblest, dearest, and best that God has. Yet the world not only failed to receive him[b] but also persecuted him more hideously than anything else that God ever sent. As in his time and at all times, only a few stand up for divine truth and risk life and limb, reputation and possessions and

129. What follows is a thinly veiled description for Luther's readers of his own experience.

130. Especially bishops and abbots or heads of orders, but Luther could mean all clergy.

b See John 1:11.

everything they have, as Christ himself promised [Matt. 24:9-10]: "Everyone will hate you for my name's sake," and "I will be a stumbling block for many." If this truth had been attacked by peasants, shepherds, stable boys, and unimportant people, who would not have been ready to profess and bear witness to it? But when the same truth is attacked by the pope and bishops along with princes and kings, everyone disappears, remains silent, and becomes a hypocrite, in order not to lose their possessions, the approval of others, their reputation, or their lives.

3. Why do people do that? Because they have no faith in God and expect from God nothing good for themselves. Where this confidence and faith are present, there is also a courageous, valiant, and dauntless heart that risks everything and stands by the truth though risking one's neck or station in life,[131] even against pope and kings, as we see that those precious martyrs once did. For such a heart remains content and gentle because it has a God that shows grace and favor, and thus it disdains the favor, graciousness, kindness, and honor coming from others, letting go of or taking in stride all transient things, as Ps. 15[:4] says: "This one despises those who despise God and honors those who fear God," that is, such a heart does not fear tyrants or the mighty who persecute the truth and despise God but disregards and despises them. At the same time, this same heart supports, stands by, watches over, and honors those who are persecuted for the truth and fear God more than human powers. It does not care who might disapprove, as Heb. 11[:27] says of Moses: "He stood by his brothers despite the mighty king of Egypt."

Look here! In this commandment, you will once again see that faith must be the master artisan[c] of this work, because without faith no one is bold enough to do it. Hence all works rest in faith, as has been said often enough. For apart from this faith all works are dead, no matter how much they gleam and call themselves good. Just as no one

---

131. German: *es gelt hals odder mantel*, literally, "it is worth neck or cloak." This unique saying in Luther is translated in the 1521 Latin version as *"sive capitis, sive pallii sit periculum"* (literally, "let there be danger to the head or cape"). The pallium often referred to a sign of episcopal office, although it could even refer to a monk's or friar's habit.

---

c   German: *Werkmeister*. See above, p. 281, note o.

This engraving is the last in a series of twelve illustrating
the consecration of a bishop. The pallium is a long
woolen cloth embroidered with six small black crosses
sent to the bishop by the pope. The ceremony of bestowal
of the pallium must take place in the new bishop's own diocese.
Here the new bishop kneels before the presiding bishop,
who places the pallium over his chasuble.

does the work of this commandment without a firm and fearless reliance on God's favor, so no one does any work of all the other commandments without this same faith. Using this commandment, individuals[d] can easily test and determine whether or not they are Christians and believe in Christ the right way and whether they do good works or not. Now we realize how the all-powerful God has placed before us our Lord Jesus Christ not only as the one in whom we should confidently believe but also as an example of this very confidence and of such good works, so that we might trust him, follow him, and abide forever in him, as he says in John 14[:6]: "I am the way, the truth, and the life," the way on which we follow him, the truth that we believe in him, and the life that we live eternally in him.

From all of this, it is now obvious that all those works that have not been commanded are perilous and easy to identify: building and decorating churches, going on pilgrimages, and all the many others that are described in detail in canon law.[132] They lead astray, burden, and corrupt the world, create anxious consciences, and they have silenced and enfeebled faith. Since people[e] have their hands full with obeying the commandments God has given, even if they used all their strength and neglected everything else, and still cannot do all these good works, why should people look for other works that are neither necessary nor commanded and ignore the ones that are?

The last two commandments,[f] which forbid the evil bodily appetites, lust, and envy of worldly goods are clear in themselves and remain in place without harming the neighbor. Even so these things remain right up to the grave, and the internal struggle against them remains until death. For that reason, in Rom. 7[:7] St. Paul merged these two com-

132. Canon law, a collection of papal and conciliar decrees, included rules for penitential acts of satisfaction.

---

d   Singular in the original.

e   Singular in the original.

f   "You shall not covet your neighbor's house; you shall not covet your neighbor's wife, or male or female slave, or ox, or donkey, or anything that belongs to your neighbor" (Exod. 20:17; Deut. 5:21).

mandments into one and set one goal for them that we do not reach but can only envision until death. No one has ever been so holy that no evil inclination was felt when the cause and the stimulus were right there. For original sin is by nature innate in us. It can be dampened but never rooted out except by bodily death, which for that reason is both useful and desirable. May God help us. Amen.

Printed at Wittenberg in the press of Melchior Lotter the Younger in the year 1520.

Image Credits

262, 285, 316, 317, 365: Courtesy of the Digital Image Archive, Pitts Theology Library, Candler School of Theology, Emory University.

318 (© photos.com): Thinkstock.

279 (SEF), 434 (Foto Marburg): Art Resource, NY.